Susan Millik

# A Kestrel
# for a Knave

**Barry Hines**

Series editor:
**Steve Eddy**

Philip Allan Updates
Market Place
Deddington
Oxfordshire
OX15 0SE

*Orders*
Bookpoint Ltd, 130 Milton Park, Abingdon, Oxfordshire, OX14 4SB
tel: 01235 827720
fax: 01235 400454
e-mail: uk.orders@bookpoint.co.uk
Lines are open 9.00 a.m.–5.00 p.m., Monday to Saturday, with a 24-hour message
answering service. You can also order through the Philip Allan Updates website:
www.philipallan.co.uk

ISBN-13: 978–1–84489–609–7
ISBN-10: 1–84489–609–9

Cover photograph reproduced by permission of Ronald Grant Archive.
Kestrel running head by Craig Churchill.

Printed by Raithby, Lawrence & Co Ltd, Leicester

*Environmental information*
The paper on which this title is printed is sourced from managed, sustainable
forests.

P00708

# Contents

## Study and revision

## Context

## Plot and structure

## Characterisation

## Themes

# Style

# Tackling the exam

# Answers

# References

# Study and revision

## Approaching the text

If you have not yet read *A Kestrel for a Knave*, approach it with an open mind, ignoring what others say for or against it. Ask anyone who has read it not to tell you the ending.

Read the novel for the first time over as short a period as possible, for maximum impact. You should find this quite easy, as it is short and consists mainly of brief episodes that make you want to go on reading to find out what happens next.

Remember, however, that the narrative is not just a succession of events. While you read you should think about other aspects of the novel that influence your response, such as:

* **Characters:** how they are presented, and how they react to each other. You learn a lot from noting what they do, what they say, how they speak (for example, Billy, his friends and family use a lot of dialect; the school teachers use Standard English), and what other people say about them.
* **Setting:** how it affects what happens in the story.
* **Structure:** for example, the novel covers the events of a single day in Billy's life, but within this structure flashbacks provide important insights into his past.
* **Themes:** these emerge as the story progresses, such as the way Billy is influenced by the natural environment.
* **Style:** Barry Hines's use of imagery in descriptive passages is one example. Another is the use of light and dark, as well as colour and sound, to highlight the background to key episodes. Short sentences (often of one word), or sentences frequently broken by punctuation, reflect slow movement, stress tension, or heighten vivid scenes.

You will be more aware of these and other details on your second reading. Try to train yourself from the start to read critically. For a high grade in the exam you must show a good understanding of the way Hines constructs the novel, as well as a detailed knowledge of the sequence of events.

# Revising the text

By revision-time you will have read *A Kestrel for a Knave*, discussed it in class and completed a number of different assignments. Effective revision involves using particular techniques that help you to consolidate the knowledge and understanding you have already developed. Here are some ideas for how to go about it:

* Organise an efficient filing system which you can use throughout the revision period. Use separate sections or folders for different topics.
* Read the text at least twice more before the exam. Start by reminding yourself of your first impressions. Make brief notes to record them for future comparison.
* Episodes are not numbered in *A Kestrel for a Knave*, so it is worth marking the start of each one with a sticker that can be removed before the exam. It will save you a lot of time during revision.
* There are only 26 episodes in the novel, so it should be possible to memorise what happens in each one.
* Consider the ways in which the first and last episodes fit into the overall structure, and particularly your response to the ending.
* Evaluate the importance of the flashbacks, and their placing in the novel.
* Think about different relationships between characters: whether they convince you and where your sympathies lie.
* Even though you probably find the story and characters the most interesting aspects of the novel, don't neglect other features, such as style and themes.
* Make sure you can spell words such as simile, metaphor, imagery and onomatopoeia, as well as the names of characters.
* Try to imagine questions that might be set in the exam. Make essay plans.
* Select quotations that appeal to you, or those you think might be useful. Learn some, and make sure you will be able to find others quickly during the exam. (For example, does Billy say, 'Is it heck tame, it's trained that's all,' in Episode 12, 15 or 20?)
* If you have the Penguin Classics edition, read Barry Hines's Afterword. He comments on the background to the novel, and talks about the making of the film *Kes*. If you are using another copy, try to borrow the Penguin Classics edition from a friend, or order it from the library.

# Making the most of this guide

This guide is designed to give you a firm basis for studying *A Kestrel for a Knave*. Here are some hints about how to use it:

* Regard it as a useful tool in your approach to the text, but not as a substitute for personal exploration of the book. Examiners soon recognise the difference

between answers based solely on a guide and those reflecting the candidate's own selection and evaluation of evidence.

* Read everything in the guide, including the background information in the Context section. A good understanding of this is necessary for a high-grade answer to some questions.

* The Plot and structure section is especially useful for quick reference. It has bullet-point reminders of main events in each episode, and brief summaries, and can be used from the start or as you progress deeper into your studies.

* Key point and Pause for thought inserts give brief background information or invite you to stop and consider an issue.

* The Characterisation section examines the most important attributes of major characters and gives short descriptions of minor ones.

* The Themes section offers one approach to analysing the themes of the novel and may stimulate other ways of thinking about them.

* Most sections include a Text focus which provides close scrutiny of a selected passage. These, and the section on Style, help you to develop your own critical skills.

* Each section ends with questions reviewing what you have learned. Check the Answers at the back of the guide.

* The section on Tackling the exam should be left until the final stage of your studies. It includes hints on answering questions and gives sample C and A* grade essays.

# Watching the film

If you can, watch the 1969 film *Kes*, made by Ken Loach and based on the novel. Available on DVD or video, it can be ordered from your public library.

The film was shot in Barnsley, near the village where Barry Hines grew up. David Bradley, who plays Billy Casper, is the son of a miner. Like Billy, David had no intention of going down the pit. In an interview in 1999 he said: 'I spent an hour in a mine as a boy and I knew I couldn't handle that kind of life. It was a gruelling existence. Looking back at my dad, I realise that each day he spent eight hours working and eight hours sleeping — that means he spent two-thirds of his hours in darkness.'

Some incidents, such as Kes flying to the lure, are more effective on the screen than on the page, but others in the book do not translate well into film, so they were omitted. The tall story is one example. Barry Hines has recalled that during filming they realised that having Billy write it took too long and led to a loss of emotional impact (Penguin Afterword).

Except for Billy's burial of Kes, which is brought forward into the early evening, the whole of the final episode is cut from the film. There is no flashback to Billy's

childhood visit to the cinema, with his father leaving home for good afterwards. Nor do we share Billy's fantasy of Kes chasing Jud over the countryside in revenge.

There are some additional scenes, such as Jud and Mrs Casper in the pub, and Jud walking down into the mine. We also see Billy reading hesitantly from a falconry book. This helps a viewer who has not read the novel to understand something about falconry, as well as Billy's reading problems.

Another change is the inclusion of girls in the school scenes. You may like to examine your own feelings about these and other adaptations made for the film. A disadvantage of watching the film is that you may mistakenly refer in the exam to incidents that don't occur in the novel. You will lose marks for this.

Find out more about the film at:

www.sensesofcinema.com/contents/cteq/03/28/kes.html
www.geocities.com/freycinette/Kes.

# Page references

This guide sees *A Kestrel for a Knave* as being divided into 26 episodes separated by line breaks. Page references are given for the Penguin Classics edition (PC) published in 2000, the 1969 Penguin edition (P) and the 1996 Heinemann New Windmill edition (H). For example P56 refers to page 56 of the Penguin edition.

# Context

> What is Barry Hines's background?
> What does he have in common with Billy Casper, the main character in the novel?
> What was the tripartite system in secondary education?
> How did the introduction of the CSE examination improve pupils' prospects?
> Why were housing estates often demoralising places to live?
> Why did a kestrel have the lowest status in the falconry hierarchy?

## Barry Hines

Barry Hines was born in 1939. He was brought up in the South Yorkshire pit village of Hoyland, near Barnsley. His father was a miner and so was his grandfather, who died down the pit. His mother was a maid in a large house. They were a loving, supportive family.

Hines passed the 11+ examination and went to a grammar school in Ecclesfield. He was a keen footballer, playing for the England Grammar Schools football team and later for Barnsley. He would have liked to turn professional. Instead, when he left school he went to Rockingham Colliery (now closed) and worked as an apprentice mining surveyor for six months.

Hines might have stayed at the mine, but a neighbour watching him crawling over the coalface asked whether he couldn't find a better job than that. Hines decided he could, and went to Loughborough Physical Training College. He then taught PE and some English, spending two years in a London comprehensive school before returning to the north.

At this point Hines began to combine teaching in the day with writing at night. His first novel, *The Blinder* (about the football world), was published in 1966. *A Kestrel for a Knave* followed in 1968. Its immediate success, and the subsequent film adaptation, *Kes*, enabled Hines to become a full-time writer of novels and plays. Since then, *A Kestrel for a Knave* has been adapted as a play and as a musical.

Hines spent two years in the 1980s as Writer in Residence at Sheffield Polytechnic, and he is now an Honorary Fellow of Sheffield Hallam University. Two novels, *The Price of Coal* (set in a pit) and *Looks and Smiles* (a teenage love

story), have recently been republished after a period out of print. The film version of *Looks and Smiles* won a prize at the Cannes Film Festival. Hines's television nuclear war drama, *Threads*, won a BAFTA award.

Hines says he wanted to write because he enjoyed novels like Alan Sillitoe's *The Loneliness of the Long Distance Runner,* which have real working men and women as their main characters (BBC interview). Much of his writing is concerned with social issues. *A Kestrel for a Knave* surveys the education system that he believes failed boys like Billy Casper. As a teacher himself, Hines speaks from first-hand experience.

Like Billy Casper, Hines lived in an area of South Yorkshire near to countryside, and spent much of his youth exploring with his friends, occasionally taking a young magpie from its nest to rear. Like Billy, he used to watch a kestrel feeding her nestlings high up in a crumbling wall. He would never have taken a fledgling, but when his younger brother was given one to rear, Hines became closely involved in its training. It is this experience, and books like T. H. White's *The Goshawk*, that made him so knowledgeable about falconry.

Find out more about Barry Hines at:

www.red-star-research.org.uk/rpm/barryhines.html

www.pomonauk.com/books/barryhines/biog.php

www.bbc.co.uk/southyorkshire/features/kes/hines.shtml

# Education in the 1960s

Education in the 1960s was shaped by the 1944 Education Act, which guaranteed free schooling for every child aged from 5 to 15 years.

The three-tier system of grammar school, secondary modern and technical school was designed to cater for all abilities. Children passing the 11+ examination, introduced at that time, no longer had to pay fees or get a scholarship to go to grammar schools. Secondary modern schools were developed for less academic pupils and, in theory, technical schools were established for those of a more practical nature.

In practice, the system was less satisfactory than it seemed. Grammar schools took about 20% of all children, but received a higher proportion of money than the others for books and equipment. There were too few technical schools, so they had an intake of about 5%, and 75% of all children, many of whom might have flourished elsewhere, went to secondary moderns.

Although late developers could take a 13+ examination for the grammar school, this rarely happened. Children who did not pass the 11+ regarded themselves, and were regarded, as failures. Many of their teachers felt the same, accepting posts at secondary moderns only because they could find nothing better. Hines recalls talking to one teacher who was moving from a secondary modern to a grammar school. The pay was the same, but he regarded his new position as promotion (Penguin Afterword).

While the curriculum in the grammar schools was broad, preparing pupils for any career they might wish to enter, the curriculum in the secondary modern schools was limited, usually offering no languages or individual sciences. Before 1965, only a few pupils in secondary moderns stayed at school until 16, studying selected subjects for the GCE 'O'-level examinations taken by all grammar school pupils.

CSEs were introduced as a less demanding alternative to 'O' levels, giving many more pupils the chance to leave school with some sort of qualification. The highest grade in a CSE was considered equal to a pass in GCE, but lower-grade CSEs could also improve a school-leaver's job prospects.

Mary Evans

Grammar school boys in the 1960s

Barry Hines does not pinpoint the year in which he sets *A Kestrel for a Knave*, but even if CSEs had been introduced in time for Billy, he would not have sat the exams. As he tells the youth employment officer, he has 'a job to read and write'. It is possible that Billy might have fared better in the comprehensive system. Introduced from the mid-1960s to replace the existing tripartite system, comprehensive schools were designed for pupils of all abilities. However, they were slow to reach the north of England. Hines regards them as 'an advance of sorts', but feels that 'the principles of comprehensive education have only been pursued in a half-hearted way' (Penguin Afterword).

Meanwhile many pupils in secondary moderns felt they were marking time as they entered their final, fourth year. With no chance to gain qualifications for future employment, they wanted to leave school, find a job and start to earn a wage. Hines recalls that many boys were sent to his local secondary modern (the model for the school in the novel) wearing boiler suits and boots because so much of the day was spent rolling around the floor fighting. Their mothers felt they might as well dress for the job, rather than spoil good clothes.

It is in this dismal setting that Billy Casper is placed. He dislikes school, has no idea what he wants to do next (except to stay out of the mine, where most local boys end up) and does not seem to care much. However, he is fortunate to live in a time of almost full employment, with many opportunities to work in factories, offices, shops, farms, in general labouring and for the council.

# Housing estates

In 1945, at the end of the Second World War, the UK had a shortage of nearly one million houses. This demand for new housing was created by war damage, slum clearance, increased expectations of a better standard of living and the expansion of the manufacturing workforce.

Planners developed housing estates on the outskirts of cities to meet this urgent need. Some estates were well designed and longlasting, but others were hastily erected and soulless, with identical houses covering wide areas of land. Many residents of the new estates were used to smaller and more crowded accommodation. While they enjoyed the increased space, they felt isolated and missed having close relationships with their neighbours.

Some estates began to deteriorate within a few years. There was not enough public money to maintain them properly, and the lack of community spirit added to the problems of upkeep. There was also widespread wilful destructiveness.

It is on one of these estates that Billy lives. Mrs Casper, a single mother at work all day, goes out in the evenings in search of company, leaving Billy alone. Before he finds Kes, he is one of the vandals who add to the neighbourhood's miseries.

# Kestrels and falconry

## Kestrels

If you have ever noticed a bird with broad pointed wings and a slim tail hovering motionless above a motorway, you have almost certainly seen a common kestrel like the one that Billy Casper finds and trains in *A Kestrel for a Knave*.

The kestrel belongs to the falcon family (*Falconidae*). The male is about 13 inches (33 cm) long, with spotted chestnut upper-parts, warm buff under-parts scattered with black spots, and a blue-grey head and tail. The female (like Kes) is slightly larger than the male, with rusty brown barred upper-parts and a rusty barred tail. The kestrel's call is a shrill repeated *kee kee kee* and a more musical double note, *kee-lee*.

The kestrel has other, vernacular names such as kes, kessie and moosie-haak (Orkney). It is sometimes called the 'motorway hawk' because it favours the undisturbed verges of motorways for hunting its prey, which mainly consists of small mammals such as mice and voles, but also small birds.

The falcon's ability to hover, apparently motionless in the sky, is the reason for another of its names, windhover. In fact it only appears stationary: it is moving slowly into the wind to stay above the exact point on the ground where it has spotted its quarry (prey) before stooping (swooping down) for the kill.

The extract below comes from a poem by Gerard Manley Hopkins (1844–89) about a kestrel. You may find his style difficult in some ways, but it is not necessary to tease out all his allusions to share his vision of the bird's uplifting spirit.

The Windhover

*To Christ our Lord*

I caught this morning morning's minion, king-

    dom of daylight's dauphin, dapple-dawn-drawn Falcon, in his riding

    Of the rolling level underneath him steady air, and striding

High there, how he rung upon the rein of a wimpling wing

In his ecstasy! then off, off forth on a swing,

    As a skate's heel sweeps smooth on a bow-bend: the hurl and gliding

    Rebuffed the big wind. My heart in hiding

Stirred for a bird, — the achieve of, the mastery of the thing!

The following extract is taken from 'The Hawk in the Rain', a poem by Ted Hughes (1930–98). He writes about a kestrel, which is, strictly speaking, a falcon, but he calls it a hawk. This is not unusual; many different birds of prey are loosely classed as hawks. You will notice that Billy Casper often refers to Kes as a hawk.

    …the hawk

Effortlessly at height hangs his still eye.

His wings hold all creation in a weightless quiet,

Steady as a hallucination in the streaming air.

Find out more about kestrels at:

www.birdsofbritain.co.uk/bird-guide/kestrel.htm

## Falconry

Falconry is the art of rearing falcons (and other birds of prey) and training them to return from a flight to a lure swung by the falconer, or to hunt quarry. Beginning in the Far East about 4,000 years ago, it gradually spread west, partly as a sport and partly as a means of providing food. It became popular in Britain in the Middle Ages.

Large birds, such as gyrfalcons, were very expensive and highly prized. They were often used instead of money in ransom exchanges, or as peace-offerings between countries. Like peregrines, they could catch animals such as rabbits, herons, rooks, pheasants, partridges and other game birds. They were favourites with the aristocracy.

While people in the lower ranks of society trained and looked after their own birds, grander households employed falconers, who were considered important

Hawk Conservancy

Flying a falcon to a lure

Piers Cavendish/Ardea

Falcony equipment

men and were highly ranked among the servants.

The kestrel had inferior status. It was said to be hard to train, and its quarry was not edible for humans. The quotation from *The Boke of St Albans* (1486) that Hines uses as his epigraph places the kestrel in the lowest position, fit only for a knave or a servant. In theory it was an offence for anyone to keep a bird of prey above his station in life, but it is not known how rigorously this law was enforced.

Falconry was the favourite sport of most English monarchs from Alfred the Great to George III. Then, in the eighteenth century, new methods of land use and agriculture, as well the growing availability of the shotgun, led to its decline.

The sport lingered on into the nineteenth century, mainly through expensive sporting clubs, but there was a resurgence of interest in the early twentieth century. Now there are falconry centres throughout the UK where visitors can watch a variety of birds being flown by experts. Those wishing to learn the art must take falconry courses and obtain a licence to own a bird. Strict laws now protect birds of prey in the wild.

In Episode 15 of *A Kestrel for a Knave* Billy Casper describes how he trained Kes, emphasising the care and patience this required. These qualities are also emphasised in T. H. White's *The Goshawk* (1951), an extract from which follows:

*Friday, Saturday, Sunday*

They were days of attack and counter-attack, a kind of sweeping to and fro across disputed battlefields. Gos had gone back a long way toward wildness with his first sleep…it was backward and forward the whole time. Sometimes he would step on to the glove after hesitation, but without temper, and sometimes he would fly away as if I had come to do him murder. We walked alone for hours every day. Gos sometimes conversing in amicable if puzzled mews, sometimes flapping and bating twice every minute. All the time there was a single commandment to be observed. Patience. There was no other weapon. In the face of all setbacks, of all stupidities, of all failures and scenes and exasperating blows across the face with his wings as he struggled, there was only one thing one could seek to do. Patience ceased to be negative, became a positive action. For it had to be active benevolence. One could torture the bird, merely by giving it a hard and bitter look.

Find out more about falconry at:

www.hawk-conservancy.org/histfalc.shtml

www.r3.org/life/articles/falconry.html

Find out more about the protection of birds at:

www.chm.org.uk/cats.asp?t=355

**Review your learning**

(Answers are given on page 80.)

1 Why did Barry Hines give up his apprenticeship in the mine?

2 To which family of birds does the kestrel belong?

3 What personal experience does Hines have of rearing a kestrel?

4 Why was a kestrel regarded in the past as a bird fit only for a knave, or a servant?

5 What do people have to do today to own and train a bird of prey?

6 Why does Hines think that children who did not go to grammar schools were disadvantaged?

7 Why was there a shortage of housing after the Second World War?

8 Which of the two extracts from the poems do you prefer? Why?

# Plot and structure

> ➤ How is the novel structured?
> ➤ What happens in each episode?
> ➤ Whose viewpoints do we share?
> ➤ What is the purpose of the flashbacks?

*A Kestrel for a Knave* covers one day in the life of Billy Casper, with flashbacks to events in the past. The narrative takes the form of 26 episodes. Most editions of the novel indicate the breaks between episodes, but there are no numbered headings. This gives the impression of time passing swiftly towards the tragic climax at the end of the day.

If you have not already done this, you will find it helpful to mark the start of each episode in the novel with a sticker, as they are not numbered in the texts. The stickers can be removed before the exam.

Barry Hines introduces the story with a quotation from a fifteenth-century manuscript listing the most appropriate birds of prey for different types of people. The eagle, the bird for an emperor, heads the list. Last is the kestrel, the best choice for a knave — a medieval name for a boy or a servant, but also a rogue.

## Episode summaries and commentaries

### Episode 1 (PC9; P7; H1)

* Early morning in a northern town in England. Spring, 1960s.
* Jud, a miner, is reluctant to get up to go to work. He takes out his frustration on Billy.

Billy, disturbed by Jud's coughs, snorts and attempts to find the warmest part of their shared bed, then urges him to get up for work when the alarm rings. In response Jud shouts at Billy, thumps him in the kidneys, takes his sweater and pulls off his bedclothes before leaving.

**Glossary**

**tha & thi** (dialect) you
**gi'o'er!** (dialect) give over! (stop it!)
**mam** (dialect) mother
**thi sen** (dialect) yourself
**thar** (dialect) you're

We are not told where the story is set, but the brothers use a northern dialect. Barry Hines, who grew up near Barnsley in South Yorkshire, would be familiar with this regional way of talking. If you are not used to it, try reading some aloud.

## Episode 2 (PC11; P9; H3)

- Billy comes down in the dark to light the fire.
- He does his paper round on foot, stealing from Mr Porter and the milkman.
- He glimpses the life of a middle-class household.

Billy lights the fire and leaves home without any breakfast. Jud has taken his bike, so he runs his paper round. Billy steals chocolate from the newsagent, and orange juice and eggs from the milkman. On his round he reads a *Dandy* comic and plays imaginative games. He watches a happy middle-class family and enviously peers into their comfortable house.

The last part of Billy's round lies on the edge of the moor above the town. The description of the view gives a clear impression of the setting of the novel.

### Glossary

**nog** a small block or peg of wood
**jamb** the side post of a doorway or window
**pumps** gym shoes or trainers
**owt** (dialect) anything
**tab** cigarette
**winding gear** a tall tower at the pit-head for raising and lowering a cage between the surface and the mine

### Pause for thought

The *Dandy* story is given in great detail. Perhaps Hines wants to suggest that Desperate Dan is Billy's hero because he is huge and strong: someone who could stand up to Jud, unlike himself.

The story is told by a third-person narrator, but we view much of Billy's environment through his own eyes. Notice how when he lights the fire he sees the newspaper balls as a bouquet of hydrangea flowers. As you read you will find many other examples of Billy's imaginative response to his environment.

## Episode 3 (PC20; P16; H12)

- Billy returns to Mr Porter's shop.

Billy hides his eggs in his pocket before entering the shop. Mr Porter greets him suspiciously. He claims he is thankful that he doesn't have to teach Billy. In revenge Billy shakes his ladder, pretending that he accidentally brushed past it and is anxiously trying to stop Mr Porter from falling.

### Glossary

**shotspread** the spread of lead pellets from a cartridge when a gun is fired

### Pause for thought

Why do you think Billy has sewn the large inner pocket into his windcheater?

## Episode 4 (PC22; P8; H14)

- Billy refuses to go shopping and escapes from the house.
- He visits Kes briefly.

Arriving home, Billy sees one of Mrs Casper's boyfriends leaving the house, and questions her closely. She tries to force him to go shopping and ask for credit. They skirmish and Billy escapes without Jud's betting slip. It is the beginning of a disastrous sequence of events. Billy takes refuge in the peaceful, well-maintained shed in which he keeps Kes, his kestrel. He pours out his resentment of his mother and Jud.

### Glossary

**tanner** six old pence (before decimal currency)
**fag** cigarette
**feinted** pretended to make a move
**biceps** upper arm muscles
**laths** thin, flat strips of wood

## Flashbacks

Often used in television and films, flashbacks take the reader or viewer out of the present and back to the past. They are an effective way of adding insights and details from a period preceding the time in which the story is set.

When *A Kestrel for a Knave* was published, flashbacks were a recent innovation in visual media, although they were already a popular device in novels. There are three flashbacks in *A Kestrel for a Knave*. Episodes 5–9 form the first of these.

### Pause for thought

Billy's relationship with his mother seems to lack affection or respect. What do you think of the way he speaks of her to Kes? What might excuse his outburst?

## Episode 5 (PC27; P21; H18)

- First flashback. The previous summer. Early Saturday morning.
- Billy, bird-nesting, sees two kestrels and their nest.
- He talks to the farmer.

There is more sparring between the two brothers when Jud accuses Billy of being unable to read or write. Billy eats Jud's snap and leaves to rouse Tibbut and MacDowall for bird-nesting. Unsuccessful, he goes alone.

The appearance of a male kestrel on the horizon, and the female emerging from its nest in the

### Glossary

**snap** lunch packet
**tweezed** held as if with tweezers
**snicket** narrow path
**ubiquitous** found everywhere
**covey** group of birds
**sapling** young tree
**undulating** rising and falling like waves
**tentacles** feelers and graspers, as on an octopus
**riding** track or path
**primaries** large flight feathers in a bird's wing
**stooped** swooped vertically down (to its prey)
**variegated** multi-coloured
**eroded** gradually worn away

Female kestrel with quarry

**Key point**

Bird-nesting was not illegal in the 1960s. Most birds were not protected until 1981. For more information about wild bird protection see:
www.birdsofbritain.co.uk/bird-guide/kestrel.htm

monastery wall, opens a new world for Billy. Fascinated, he watches the handover of quarry (prey) for the nestlings. The farmer, initially suspicious of Billy's intentions and concerned for the birds, is at first unwelcoming but then relents. He says the wall is overdue for demolition. This seemingly unimportant comment has more significance than we realise at the time. They discuss falconry and the farmer advises Billy to find out more at the library.

## Episode 6 (PC40; P32; H31)

* First flashback continued. Afternoon on the same day.
* Denied a falconry book at the library, Billy steals one from the bookshop.

Billy is not allowed to borrow a library book or even read one inside the library, because he is not a member. As he is not prepared to wait until Monday, which would be his first opportunity to bring back his signed membership form and join the library, he steals *A Falconer's Handbook* from a bookshop.

**Glossary**

ornithology the study of birds

**Pause for thought**

This is the third time Billy steals something. Think about his motives on each occasion and decide how he might defend himself if challenged.

## Episode 7 (PC43; P35; H34)

- First flashback continued. That evening.
- Jud continues his persecution of Billy.
- Jud and Mrs Casper prepare to go out for the night. Billy reads.

Billy has read almost half his book. Jud throws it across the room. Mocking Billy for trying to read, and for his plan to train a kestrel, he forces him to say where the nest is. Billy has to get his own tea while Mrs Casper and Jud prepare to go out. Their conversation reveals an uneasy relationship. Mrs Casper shows little interest in Billy's plans.

### Glossary

**giz** (dialect) give
**half-nelson** a hold in which a wrestler puts an arm under an opponent's arm from behind and pushes on the back of their neck
**anyroad** (dialect) anyway
**summat** (dialect) something
**florin** two old shillings (before decimal currency)

### Pause for thought

For someone accused of being unable to read, Billy is making good progress, though it does not come easily. What does this suggest about his character?

## Episode 8 (PC49; P39; H39)

- First flashback continued. Late that night.
- Jud, very drunk, finds it difficult to climb the stairs or look after himself.
- Billy attacks him when he is asleep and leaves the house.

Jud returns drunk. Incapable of getting undressed, he makes Billy help him. With Jud safely asleep, Billy vents his disgust in a vindictive attack. Jud wakes and Billy escapes into the night.

### Pause for thought

Billy's assault shows him in a new light. What does his squealing 'softly in fear and excitement' suggest about his feelings?

## Episode 9 (PC51; P41; H42)

- Flashback continued. Later the same night.
- At Monastery Farm Billy selects the strongest nestling.

### Key point

Billy's walk to Monastery Farm, which is about to change his life, tells us a lot about him. On arrival, his ascent of the wall shows his common sense and his physical fitness.

Billy returns to Monastery Farm, examines the wall carefully and climbs up to the nest. Choosing the strongest and most developed young kestrel, he takes her home in his inner pocket.

## Glossary

**waxing curve** the curved, visible part of the moon between its new and full phases
**piebald** patterned with irregular patches of black and white
**lintel** a frame of stone or wood across the top of a door or window
**crabbing** moving sideways
**meandering** winding to and fro
**eyas** a young falcon or hawk, especially one taken from a nest for training in falconry

## Episode 10 (PC54; P44; H45)

* The present. Before and during morning school.
* Billy leaves Kes and goes to school.
* He interrupts the morning register.

Billy sets off for school. His interruption during the register slips out unintentionally, but he still gets into trouble. The boys enjoy Billy's discomfort.

**Key point**

The shipping forecast is a radio bulletin about the weather at sea. German Bight is one of the areas mentioned, and it comes immediately after Fisher in the list. Billy claims he likes the sound of the names, but he may also listen to the broadcast every night out of loneliness.

## Episode 11 (PC56, P46; H47)

* Morning assembly.
* Mr Gryce, the headmaster, shouts at the boys.
* MacDowall is picked out for coughing.
* Billy feels sleepy during the Lord's Prayer.

Mr Gryce shouts at the boys for coughing and throat-clearing during assembly. He makes Mr Crossley identify a solitary cougher, MacDowall, who is sent out. Gryce threatens unnamed penalties if the singing does not improve. Billy, very tired, closes his eyes and yawns during the prayer.

### Glossary

**dirge** a lament for the dead

**Pause for thought**

The hymn chosen for this assembly concerns love and starting each day afresh. The Bible reading from Matthew 18:10 describes Jesus urging listeners to respect children, comparing this with a shepherd seeking a lost sheep and bringing it back to the fold. To what extent do you think Gryce follows these teachings?

## Episode 12 (PC59; P48; H50)

* Second flashback. Some time in the past six months.
* Billy takes Kes, now almost trained, out on the estate.

By this time Billy has trained Kes to accept a swivel and leash. His handling of her shows his competence and self-confidence, while the carefully maintained shed shows the pleasure and pride he takes in his pastime. Out on the estate he tells a child on a tricycle that kestrels like eating small boys.

    Find pictures of falconry equipment at: http://mysite.wanadoo-members.co.uk/thefalconrysuppliers/furniture.htm Then select the icons: Furniture and Falconry kits.

### Glossary

**mutes** droppings
**crozzled** (dialect) blackened at the edges
**gauntlet** a falconer's long-sleeved leather glove
**jesses** (singular, jess) short straps placed around the legs of a hawk in the early training stages
**swivel** a link of metal loops to attach jesses to the leash
**bated** fluttered and panicked
**misdemeanours** offences
**talons** claws

## Episode 13 (PC63; P51; H53)

* The present. Later during assembly.
* Billy, accused of falling asleep, is promised a thrashing.
* Three smokers are to report to Gryce's office.

Having slipped into a daydream, Billy is embarrassed to be rebuked publicly. Mr Gryce shows pleasurable anticipation of thrashing him. Three smokers are told to report to Gryce's office. Corporal punishment was an accepted part of boys' school life in the 1960s. Many parents did protest, but it was still legal.

### Pause for thought

See the section on kestrels and falconry in the Context chapter. Compare Billy's handling of Kes with his teachers' treatment of their pupils.

## Episode 14 (PC65; P53; H55)

* After assembly.
* A messenger joins the boys waiting for Mr Gryce.
* Gryce calls them in, lectures them and finds smoking equipment.
* He beats them all.

### Glossary

**paraphernalia** miscellaneous belongings
**broddling** (dialect) poking
**prioll** a card game
**peripheral** on the edge

Waiting for Gryce, Billy and MacDowall exchange insults. They agree to settle the matter at break. The messenger is forced to take the smokers' incriminating evidence.

Gryce arrives and refuses to hear the messenger. Comparing the present generation of boys unfavourably with those he first taught, he declares that there has been no advance in discipline, decency or morals since he joined the school.

In the beating the innocent messenger comes off worst, as he has not learned to cup his hands and relax. He cries and is sick on the floor.

**Pause for thought** ⏸

Gryce says he has been at the school for ten years. If it is no better than on the day it opened, what does this suggest about his time as headmaster?

## Episode 15 (PC72; P58; H62)

* Mr Farthing's English lesson is based on fact and fiction.
* Billy tells Mr Farthing and the class about training Kes.
* Told to write a tall story, Billy describes a day when everything is perfect.

Billy, sore after his beating, does not listen to the English lesson. He is instructed to follow Anderson's factual talk about tadpoles with an account of his own, and Tibbut urges him to talk about his hawk. Billy gives an enthralling account of training Kes. He is applauded by the boys and praised by Farthing.

Billy's tall story is about a day that exists only in his imagination. Written in halting English, with many errors, it describes the kind of day that is beyond his own hopes, but which many boys take for granted.

## Glossary

**leash** a leather thong fastened by a swivel to the jesses
**creance** a long line which can be wound up at one end
**temperamental** erratic and moody
**lure** a leather weight with bait attached tied to the end of a cord and swung around
**missen** (dialect) myself
**peregrinations** wanderings

Ronald Grant Archive

Billy with Kes in the film

Read from the paragraph starting, 'Right, facts. Factual accounts' (PC86; P70; H76) to the end of Billy's tall story.

> Examine the differences between Mr Farthing's and Mr Gryce's attitudes to the boys.

> Farthing's use of the class name, 4C, gives us useful information: that Billy is in the lowest group in the fourth year (which would now be called Year 10). Think about the ways in which the dictionary exercise and Billy's tall story are used to illustrate the pupils' poor basic skills.

> Look for the ways in which Farthing's tall story is slanted to include Billy's interests.

> Note how Billy's tall story says much more about himself and his home life than he realises.

> Notice how Farthing moves at the boys' pace, expanding, reaffirming and explaining the task clearly.

> Why does Barry Hines include the detailed list of activities before the boys write their stories?

> The tall story is reproduced exactly as Billy wrote it. Go through it carefully, examining the mis-spellings. Think about the way Hines presents them and how your version might differ if you were the author of the novel.

> If you were Farthing, to what extent would you correct Billy's story before handing it back?

## Episode 16 (PC90; P3; H79)

* Morning break.
* Billy and MacDowall fight.
* Billy confides in Mr Farthing.

Billy, going to the bicycle shed at break, encounters MacDowall, who insults him and his family. Billy attacks him, but is worsted on the coke pile. Mr Farthing pulls MacDowall off Billy, and shows MacDowall what it is like to be bullied.

### Glossary

**Coke** solid fuel derived from coal and used in heating boilers

Billy confides in Farthing. He is always picked on, even by the police, though he has not been in trouble since finding Kes. Billy is realistic about his limited job prospects, but hopes that when he is working he may be able to save up for a goshawk. Farthing asks if he can watch Billy flying Kes. This episode (like Episode 15) gives us new insights into Billy. He has now found someone in whom he can confide, and who seems genuinely interested in his welfare.

## Episode 17 (PC105; P85; H94)

- The washroom after the fight.
- Billy is warm and relaxed as he dreamily plays with soap bubbles in the washroom.

Study the descriptive language in this episode, especially the use of imagery. Do you think there is any connection between the bubbles and Billy's need to escape his drab life?

### Glossary
**Bisto Kid** a character in a gravy-mix advertisement
**membrane** (here) thin skin of foam
**spectrum** band of colours as seen in a rainbow

## Episode 18 (PC106; P86; H95)

- Late morning. The changing-room and playing field.
- Billy plays in goal for Mr Sugden's team.

Billy is forced by Mr Sugden to wear outsize shorts. Among the last to be chosen, he plays in goal for Sugden's team. Sugden viciously kicks a ball at Billy for failing to save a goal. Billy amuses himself playing imaginative games. A dog invades the pitch, terrifying everyone except Billy, who leads it away. Only Sugden plays seriously until the match runs into the lunch hour. Then the boys grow more competitive. Billy deliberately lets in the final goal.

### Glossary
**Hobson's choice** the choice of taking what is offered, or nothing (named after Hobson, a seventeenth-century carrier who had horses for hire and insisted that customers took the horse nearest the door)
**portal** doorway or gate
**Thalidomide** a drug taken by pregnant women in the 1950s and early 1960s, which was found to cause deformities (including loss or drastic shortening of limbs) in their babies

### Key point
After Sugden's decision that the next goal will decide the match, Barry Hines inserts a deliberate misquotation from *Vitaï Lampada* (Latin for 'the torch of life'), Henry Newbolt's famous poem about a cricket match. The original line is 'Ten to make and the match to win'.

## Episode 19 (PC127; P103; H115)

- Lunchtime. Billy dresses without taking a shower.
- Mr Sugden makes him have one.

Caught by Mr Sugden, Billy is made to have a shower and is forced to stand under the cold water jets. This is Sugden's revenge for the unsaved final goal.

### Glossary
**chassé** a dance movement
**the Final Solution** the extermination of Jews attempted by Nazi Germany in the Second World War

## Episode 20 (PC134; P108; H122)

* Billy goes home.
* He takes Jud's money and betting slip.
* He flies Kes in the field, watched by Mr Farthing.

Billy returns home to feed Kes and gambles on whether to take Jud's coins. Pocketing them, he shoots a sparrow and takes Kes out to fly on the lure. Mr Farthing arrives. He is impressed by Kes, and by Billy's skill. They discuss the special qualities of hawks.

### Glossary
**scro(a)med** (dialect) wriggled down
**feake** scrape clean

### Pause for thought
**Billy has a natural affinity with animals, yet he seems unaffected by killing the sparrow and feeding it to Kes. Does this surprise you?**

## Episode 21 (PC149; P121; H137)

* Billy decides not to place Jud's bet.
* He spends the money on himself and Kes.

Billy gambles again on whether to place Jud's bet, and loses. He asks about Jud's chance of a double. Told it is unlikely, he decides to spend the money on himself and Kes, but he is not charged by the butcher. This episode is a major turning point in the novel. By failing to place Jud's bet, and spending the money, Billy triggers the events leading to Kes's death.

### Glossary
**studying form** studying horse-racing records and prospects
**the five thousand** a reference to the Bible story of Jesus feeding five thousand people with five loaves and two fishes (St John 6: 5–14)

## Episode 22 (PC155; P126; H143)

* Afternoon school. Jud comes looking for Billy, who hides.
* As a consequence, Billy is late for his employment interview.

### Glossary
**Yale** a type of lock that can be opened without a key from the inside but not the outside

Jud comes to the school and searches for Billy. At lesson changeover Billy runs away, with Jud following him. He hides in several places before joining his classmates in the corridor. He learns that he has missed his employment interview. Seeing Billy, Mr Gryce furiously sends him to the medical room, where the interviews are being held.

## Episode 23 (PC166; P135; H153)

* Billy attends his interview with the youth employment officer, leaving early.
* He discovers that Kes is missing.

Awaiting his interview, Billy plays games to pass the time. He listens passively to the youth employment officer, participating only to point out his unsuitability for office work and state his determination not to be a miner. The reference to hobbies rouses him and he asks to go. Running home, he discovers that Kes is missing. He searches without success for Jud or Kes.

**Glossary**

**your cards** People starting work were allotted National Insurance cards. These recorded compulsory payments for sickness and unemployment benefits, and contributions towards a pension. When they changed jobs their cards were returned to them to give to their next employer.

## Episode 24 (PC174; P142; H162)

* Evening. Billy discovers the result of the horse race.
* He continues his search for Kes, to no avail.
* Returning home, he learns that Jud has killed her.

**Glossary**

**welcher** someone who fails to honour an agreement

Mrs Rose at the betting shop describes Jud's fury on discovering his bet had not been placed. In pouring rain Billy desperately goes on looking for Kes. He sees the demolished wall at Monastery Farm. When he goes home, Jud admits killing Kes, though he only meant to release her. Mrs Casper is angry about the unplaced bet and does not comfort Billy. Billy gets the dead bird out of the dustbin.

**Key point**

Now that the wall has been knocked down, Billy will not be able to find another kestrel to replace Kes.

## Episode 25 (PC185; P150; H172)

* Billy shows Kes's corpse to his mother.
* Attacking her and Jud, he runs from the house.

Billy takes Kes inside and demands justice, but his mother cannot help. Frustrated, he knocks away her teacup and attacks Jud, who swings him over his head. Brandishing Kes's body at them, Billy flees.

## Episode 26 (PC187; P153; H175)

* Night. Billy breaks into a cinema.
* Flashback. He recalls an earlier cinema visit.
* The present. He buries Kes and goes to bed.

Billy wanders around the estate until he reaches the City Road. Breaking into a derelict cinema, he sits in the auditorium recalling, in a flashback, a visit to the

same cinema with his father and their return home to find Uncle Mick with his mother, and then his father leaving home.

Back in the present he imagines Billy the Hero projected on to the screen, with Kes pursuing and stooping on Jud. He leaves the cinema, returning home to bury Kes and go to bed.

# Timeline

| Flashbacks | Episodes | Main narrative | Page numbers |
|---|---|---|---|
| | | A day in spring | |
| | 1 | Early morning. Jud's alarm call. | PC9; P7; H1 |
| | 2 | Billy does his paper round. | PC11; P9; H3 |
| | 3 | He returns to Mr Porter's shop. | PC20; P16; H12 |
| | 4 | Billy refuses to shop for his mother or to take Jud's betting slip. | PC22; P18; H14 |
| A Saturday the previous summer.Early morning. Billy sees the kestrels at Monastery Farm. | 5 | | PC27; P21; H18 |
| Afternoon.The library and the bookshop. | 6 | | PC40; P32; H31 |
| Evening. Billy reads his falconry book. | 7 | | PC43; P35; H34 |
| Night. Jud returns very drunk. Billy goes out. | 8 | | PC49; P39; H39 |
| Billy takes a young kestrel from its nest. | 9 | | PC51; P41; H42 |
| | 10 | Morning school. Billy interrupts Mr Crossley taking the register. | PC54; P44; H45 |
| | 11 | Billy starts to feel sleepy during assembly. | PC56; P46; H47 |
| Some months later. Billy takes Kes round the estate. | 12 | | PC59; P48; H50 |

| Flashbacks | Episodes | Main narrative | Page numbers |
|---|---|---|---|
| | 13 | Billy is caught dozing in assembly. | PC63; P51; H53 |
| | 14 | Mr Gryce thrashes Billy and some other boys. | PC65; P53; H55 |
| | 15 | The English lesson and tall story. | PC72; P58; H62 |
| | 16 | Morning break. The fight. Billy confides in Mr Farthing. | PC90; P73; H79 |
| | 17 | Billy plays with water in the washroom. | PC105; P85; H94 |
| | 18 | The football match. | PC106; P86; H95 |
| | 19 | Lunchtime. Mr Sugden's revenge in the shower room. | PC127; P103; H115 |
| | 20 | Billy collects Jud's betting slip and money. Mr Farthing watches him fly Kes. | PC134; P108; H122 |
| | 21 | Billy spends Jud's money on food for himself and Kes. | PC149; P121; H137 |
| | 22 | Afternoon school. Jud searches the school. Billy is late for his youth employment interview. | PC155; P126; H143 |
| | 23 | The youth employment interview and Billy's dash home to find Kes. | PC166; P135; H153 |
| | 24 | Evening. Billy searches for Kes, confronts Jud and learns the truth. | PC174; P142; H162 |
| | 25 | Billy attacks Mrs Casper and Jud, and runs off. | PC185; P150; H172 |
| The distant past. Billy recalls a visit to the cinema, and his father leaving home. | 26 | Night. Billy breaks into the cinema, returns home, buries Kes, and goes to bed. | PC187; P153; H175 |

# Structure

*A Kestrel for a Knave* focuses on a single day in the life of 15-year-old Billy Casper. It follows the events of the day in chronological order, starting with Billy in bed early in the morning and concluding with him back in his bleak bedroom at night.

The story is told by a third-person narrator, though we see much through Billy's eyes, especially his surroundings. But we also share Barry Hines's personal outlook, and his views on education.

There are no chapters. Instead, the story is told in a series of 26 episodes. This suits the short time span and reflects the rapid and inexorable progress of events.

Each episode deepens our understanding of Billy: as a vulnerable, deprived teenager; a natural victim; a petty thief; a lover of nature; a slow learner; a skilful falconer; a natural comic; a no-hoper and a desolate mourner of Kes.

The disadvantage of such a short novel is that there is limited scope to develop characters in detail or set events in a wider context. Barry Hines compensates for this with three flashbacks to the past.

## Pause for thought

**What other aspects of Billy emerge as we read the book? Make a list that you can use in your revision. Include those listed here.**

## Key point

**In families with low incomes and small houses it was a common practice for siblings to share beds. For this to work well, they needed to be on good terms, but the opening scene in Hines's novel establishes tension between Billy and Jud even before they wake.**

The novel opens on a spring morning with Billy in bed with Jud. By the end of the day, Jud has destroyed all that Billy holds dear.

The first four episodes establish the setting of the novel and introduce the Casper family. Billy is not spared criticism. We learn of his attractive qualities, such as his observant nature and imaginative games on his paper round, but also of his failings, such as lying and stealing.

Barry Hines introduces Jud's betting slip and money early in the story (Episode 4). It seems unimportant at the time, but it is the start of the trail that leads directly to the death of Kes.

The first flashback, in Episodes 5–9, shows different aspects of Billy: his interest in the natural world and the environment, and his determination to train a kestrel. Mirroring the structure of the main narrative, it is a chronological account of one Saturday the previous summer. Starting with Billy's early rise to go bird-nesting, it ends late at night on his return with a baby kestrel.

Hines brings us back to the present at the start of Episode 10 with Billy visiting Kes before school.

Episodes 10 and 11 are mostly concerned with conditions in secondary modern schools, revealing Billy as one of the many victims of the system. The description of the inferior teachers, their methods and attitudes, redeemed only by Mr Farthing, reflects Hines's concern that many children received few benefits from their education.

Billy's dozing off in assembly leads into his daydream in the second flashback (Episode 12). Set at some time during the past six months, it focuses on Billy's short walk round the estate with Kes. Its purpose is to show how much Billy has achieved since he started training her.

Like the main narrative and the first flashback, Billy's tall story (Episode 15) is another account of a full day. In some ways it is at the heart of the novel. Coming immediately after his talk to the class about Kes, which also gives fresh insight into his character, the tall story paints a touching picture of Billy's desires and feelings. It starts with breakfast in bed served by his attentive and affectionate mother, after which Billy learns the welcome news that Jud has joined the army but his father is coming home. It then describes Billy at school with kindly teachers, coming home to a mother who has decided not to go out to work any more, going to the pictures with his mother and father in the evening, and finally having a fish and chip supper before going to bed.

Presented as Billy writes it, without corrections, the story reveals his weak writing skills and shows just how hard he must have worked to master the difficult and complex subject of falconry.

Except for the final flashback, the story continues with a sequence of events that lead inexorably to the terrible climax. We are with Billy in morning school, at break, at lunchtime, in afternoon school, in his search for Kes and the discovery that she is dead, and at night when he roams around the estate and breaks into the cinema. The low-key ending, when Billy quietly returns home to bury Kes and go to bed, is far more poignant than a dramatic conclusion. We feel that, drained of emotion, he has no more fight left in him.

The final flashback is embedded in the last episode. Breaking into the cinema, Billy recalls an evening with his father some years ago that started happily and ended with his father leaving home. It is an important point in the novel, because it explains why Mr Casper left home and shows just how much Billy has lost. It also suggests how differently he might have developed with a loving father to guide him.

Billy's tall story of a perfect day in Episode 15 makes his father's return home a highlight. We may have guessed why his father left home when Billy was young, but Hines holds back from telling us until the final episode, when Billy recalls his departure. It was then that everything started to go wrong for Billy, and perhaps Hines is making the point that Billy has been here before. For the second time in

his young life he has lost, suddenly and unexpectedly, the focus of his love and affection. Once again the prospect is dismal.

It seems, at the end, that there is nothing much left for Billy. He has lost Kes, his mother shows little sympathy, and he surely hates Jud more then ever. About to leave school and exchange one place he dislikes for another, he has no illusions about his future. Hines does, however, suggest a faint light in the darkness. Billy tells Mr Farthing (Episode 16) that he has been reading about goshawks and might be able to save his pay to buy one to train. Perhaps, one day, Billy will achieve this.

### Review your learning

(Answers are given on page 80.)

1  Why is the novel written in short episodes rather than longer chapters?
2  What is the purpose of the flashbacks?
3  Which episode is the major turning point in the novel?
4  What is an eyas?
5  What does Billy buy with Jud's betting money?
6  What does Billy think he may save up for when he starts work?
7  Who says: 'You won't half cop it, lad, when he gets hold of you'?
8  Billy says 'There's allus somebody after me though'. Why do you think this is so, and does he deserve it?
9  A friend asks you to recommend two episodes as a foretaste, before deciding whether to read the whole novel. Which of the following would you select, and why? Episode 2; Episode 5; Episode 15; Episode 18; Episode 20; Episode 26.

# Characterisation

➢ Who are the characters?
➢ What are they like?
➢ What part do they play in the plot?

Note: the numbers in brackets refer to episodes in the novel.

## Billy Casper

* is 15 years old and in his final year at a secondary modern school
* is small and immature for his age and cries easily
* lives on a dismal housing estate with a bad reputation
* is undernourished and permanently cold
* has an unhappy relationship with his mother, lacking affection or respect
* hates his brother Jud, who constantly bullies him
* misses his father
* is happiest in the countryside, with nature and animals as his companions
* finds a purpose in life with Kes
* is considered stupid and a nuisance at school
* is a victim of bullying by staff and boys
* is resilient in tackling the problems of daily life
* is determined not to go down the mine

### Billy says

* 'I've never taken owt o'yours, have I?' (2)
* 'Then it dived down behind that wall and came up wi' summat in its claws. You ought to have seen it, mister, it wa' smashin'.' (5)
* 'Well that was it. I'd done it. I'd trained her.' (15)
* 'I seem to get into bother for nowt.' (16)
* 'Do you know, Sir, I feel as though she's doin' me a favour just lettin' me stand here.' (20)
* 'I wouldn't be seen dead down t'pit.' (23)
* 'What about him though? What you goin' to do to him? I want you to do summat to him.' (25).

### Commentary

Billy is a fully rounded character so that, unlike 'flat' characters whose responses are always predictable, we are never quite certain how he will react to events.

Although the story is told by a third-person narrator, we see Billy's world through his own eyes.

Billy is not exactly the hero of the novel; he is more of an anti-hero (the central character in a novel, play, etc. who lacks the traditional heroic virtues). We can see him as a victim of circumstances, since his family life, the estate he lives on and his education give him little chance to develop into an outgoing, law-abiding teenager.

In his Afterword to the Penguin Classics edition of the novel, Barry Hines says that Billy is not based on a real person, though as 'the lonely misfit who doesn't belong to the gang' he is not unusual. His life is tough, with 'the odds stacked against him'. Hines also says that Billy is not presented as a feeble, blameless character whom everybody picks on. 'This would have weakened and sentimentalised the story. Billy is a survivor, a tough little character, more Artful Dodger than Oliver Twist.'

Billy appears to be a failure: only semi-literate, in the lowest stream of his year in a secondary modern school, with a police record and little to look forward to. Finding Kes leads to the discovery of his other qualities.

Billy may never have had many friends, but he has fewer since deserting the gang for Kes. His house is cold and untidy (in contrast to the cosy home he has made for Kes), the larder is often empty, his mother is frequently out in the evening, his father has gone and he hates Jud, so he has no source of adult guidance. Billy's tall story (15) and the flashback to the cinema visit (26) show how much he misses his father and yearns for a better life.

Billy's relationship with his mother lacks affection or respect, but this is not surprising, since she is self-centred and uncaring. When Billy turns to her for comfort after Kes's death, she rebuffs him (25).

In some ways Billy is not likeable. He steals from Mr Porter and the milkman (2), the bookshop (6) and Jud (21). He lies to Mr Porter about stealing (2), to Mr Farthing about where he found Kes (15), to Mr Sugden about the shower (19), and to Mr Gryce when caught in the corridor (22). He throws missiles when he is angry (at his mother and Mrs MacDowall), and takes advantage of Jud's drunken sleep to attack him viciously (8). Billy is also rude to his mother (4 and 24), and impertinent to Sugden (19) and Gryce (22).

In spite of these failings, however, Billy retains our sympathy, partly because we feel he is the product of his upbringing, and partly because there is a different side to him.

He is at home in the fields and woods, and knows how to handle animals, as when he strokes the young thrushes' backs (5) or gently leads the dog off the football pitch (18). In his handling and training of Kes he is patient, competent and knowledgeable. As he explains to Farthing, she is not a pet; he respects her and knows he cannot tame her: 'Is it heck tame, it's trained that's all. It's fierce and it's wild' (20). His practical approach to animals is shown when he kills the sparrow for Kes (20).

WOODFALL FILMS present
A KESTREL FILMS PRODUCTION
" K E S "ᵤ
Starring DAVID BRADLEY
From BARRY HINES' Book "KESTREL FOR A KNAVE"
TECHNICOLOR ✦        UNITED ARTISTS

Ronald Grant Archive

Billy makes great efforts to overcome his literacy problems so he can read falconry books (7 and 20). He is observant and sensitive to his natural surroundings, examining the dew on a blade of grass and a scrape of moss while bird-nesting (5), and answering a tawny owl's cry (9).

He is imaginative, perceiving other shapes in the paper and kindling for the fire (2). To him, the woods at night are a curtain stretching up to the sky, with the trunks and branches of the trees as terrace doorways (9). He invents games to amuse himself on his paper round (2), in the washroom (17), on the games field (18), and while awaiting his youth employment interview (23).

Billy is also a natural comic. Farthing cannot help laughing when Billy impersonates a stern teacher (16).

He shows his practical skills in such activities as laying the fire (2), preparing and maintaining the shed (7 and 12), and learning to handle, as well as make, hawking equipment.

Since finding Kes, Billy no longer gets into trouble, but he has a police record. He tells Farthing that the police still come to his house to question him and confesses that he feels like 'goin' out an' doin' summat just to spite 'em sometimes' (16). Instead, he spends evenings in the shed with Kes (7, 12, 20).

When Billy gives his class a description of training and flying Kes (15) we see a knowledgeable, confident and relaxed side of him. Before this he has been treated as an outsider by most of the boys, but their attitude towards him changes subtly after his talk and they sympathise when Sugden ill-treats him (18 and 19).

Sugden's main reason for disliking Billy is that he does not enjoy organised games, but with encouragement he might be a good footballer, as he is fit and agile. He runs his paper round (2), scales the pine tree (5) and the monastery wall (9), climbs on to the goal crossbar (18), clambers out of the showers (19), swings the lure while balanced on a stile (24) and climbs through the cinema window (26).

In school, Billy is regularly beaten, for instance after dozing in assembly (13), and is regarded as a persistent troublemaker. He claims to Farthing that he is no worse than most of the other boys (16).

Billy's fight with MacDowall starts outside Gryce's office (14), then erupts fully when MacDowall remarks that Billy has more 'uncles' than most boys and suggests that Jud is not a 'right brother' (16). It is not clear if Billy has suspected this, but he is sensitive to comments about his family.

Billy's conversation with Farthing (16) is one of the few occasions when he openly expresses his feelings (26). Apart from the farmer, Farthing may be the first person in years to show a genuine interest in him.

Billy's initial refusal to take Jud's betting slip (4) and his later decision not to place the bet (21) may be the wrong things to do, but they are understandable, given Jud's unkindness to Billy. The betting money enables Billy to buy some lunch (which he desperately needs, having had no dinner or breakfast) and some food for Kes. He is short of money himself because most of his earnings from the paper round go towards outstanding police fines. Whatever we feel about Billy's actions, their outcome is disastrous, as they lead to the destruction of Kes.

At his interview with the youth employment officer Billy seems uninterested in his future (23). He is probably worrying about what Jud plans to do next. He knows his limitations. 'I shall take what they've got,' he has told Mr Farthing earlier (16). He is more direct with his interviewer: 'I'd be all right working in an office, wouldn't I? I've a job to read and write.' Billy is certain of only one thing: he does not intend to be a miner.

### Pause for thought

Do you think that Billy underestimates his own abilities? He has made great strides since he worked laboriously through his first falconry book. Perhaps with better teaching and greater motivation at school he might have improved his writing skills. But it is too late now.

Billy's desperate search for Kes, and his rage and despair when he learns her fate (24), show just how much the bird meant to him. The fact that he later roams the estate and breaks into the cinema (26) is a worrying suggestion that he will now return to his former way of life. Meanwhile, his quiet return home and burial of Kes suggest that he has smothered his anguish, knowing there is nothing more to be done. There is no comfort now, but perhaps in due course he will focus on realising the dream he confided to Mr Farthing (16): saving up to buy a goshawk.

Read carefully from the start of Episode 20 ('Home, straight home') to 'Come on, Kes! Come on then!' Referring closely to the text, note the following points:

➤ Kes's response to Billy's clucking tongue shows how much he has achieved. She is as relaxed with him as a wild bird can be in captivity. When he returns to the shed a little later with the dead sparrow, she screams and eagerly presses her face against the bars.

➤ The description of the breadboard, with its gleaming steel blade, reveals Billy's meticulous approach to Kes's care. Aware of the dangers of infection in captive birds, he sniffs the beef carefully before placing it in his satchel.

➤ The description of the living room, with curtains still drawn and clothes littered over the furniture, confirms our earlier impressions of Mrs Casper's neglectful nature.

➤ Billy's method of deciding whether to take Jud's money shows that he likes to gamble.

➤ Air rifles use just one slug at a time, yet Billy hits his target perfectly. Although the telescopic sights help him to focus, he is clearly a good shot. He does not leave anything to chance when shooting birds for Kes. The carefully placed, permanently marked chalk cross gives him the best view from both windows of the shed, and he waits patiently until the right moment to fire at the sparrow.

➤ The description of the doomed sparrow 'curving up over the gutter like an egg in a cup' reflects Billy's imaginative nature.

➤ When Kes tenses outside the shed Billy does not try to hurry her, but waits for her to relax and resume feeding.

➤ Earlier, Billy described to his class how he trained Kes. The vivid description of them both in action makes it easier to visualise, and to understand more clearly the skills Billy has mastered.

✳ On what other occasion does Billy gamble?

✳ What does Billy need to take with him when he flies Kes?

✳ The names of the horses seem to have an ominous ring. Is Billy a 'Crackpot' if he doesn't place Jud's bet? Does 'Tell Him He's Dead' have sinister implications?

✳ Make brief notes summarising what you have learned about Billy from this extract. Keep them for later revision.

# Jud

- is Mrs Casper's son, but has a different surname
- lives with Billy and Mrs Casper in their home on Valley Estate
- is known as 't'cock o't'estate' (16)
- is quick-tempered and a bully, frequently abusing Billy verbally and physically
- uses crude language and swears frequently
- is a miner
- takes every opportunity to belittle Billy's abilities and interests
- kills Kes

## Jud says

- 'What's up wi' thee, shit t'bed?' (5)
- 'Hawks are a menace to farmers, they eat all their poultry an' everything.' (7)
- 'Hel' me ge' undresh, Billy. Am pish. Am too pish to take my trouser off.' (8)
- 'It's his fault! If he'd have put that bet on like he wa' told there'd have been none o'this!' (24)
- 'Ten quid. I could have had a week off work wi' that.' (24)

## Commentary

The presentation of Jud is flatter than that of Billy: we see only one side of his character. He is foul-mouthed, fiery-tempered and bullies Billy both verbally and physically. If Billy is the anti-hero, Jud is the villain.

Jud appears in Episodes 1, 7, 8, 22, 24 and 25. His first words and actions are representative of everything he says and does. He ill-treats Billy in the bedroom, takes his shirt (1), drinks all the milk and takes his bike (2). Later, having belittled Billy's reading skills and his intention of training a kestrel, Jud attacks Billy viciously when he refuses to say where the kestrel is (7). Jud's threat to shoot Kes is probably made just to frighten Billy, but with hindsight it seems an ominous foreshadowing of events. In spite of this treatment, Jud expects Billy to run his errands and to undress him when he arrives home drunk (8).

Jud's lack of respect and affection for his mother are reflected in his unpleasant insinuation about her boyfriends, his reference to her frequent drunken behaviour (7) and his threatening attitude when Billy appeals to her for support (25). His hypocrisy is demonstrated by the fact that he too is promiscuous and drinks heavily, going out on Saturday nights to get drunk and find a 'bird' (7). His violent and vengeful tendencies are illustrated by his behaviour in the betting office, his rampage through the school in search of Billy (22), and his attempted release and eventual killing of Kes (24). He shows no remorse for this act and does not apologise, saying instead that the bird is worth less than the £10 he has lost (24).

In his defence, we should remember that Jud, like Billy, has been shaped by his background and environment. He may never have known his father, and probably resented Billy's birth. He has a hard life as a miner, perhaps hating it as much as Billy dreads it. He finds escape in drink and betting, and realises that he could have had a week's holiday with the money Billy lost him. We should also remember that he does not set out to kill Kes. Scratched and torn by her talons in his attempt to release her, he reacts by wringing her neck.

**Pause for thought**

To what extent do you think that Jud's behaviour is justified?

Billy and Jud fight while Mrs Casper looks on

# Mrs Casper

- is Jud's and Billy's mother
- was unfaithful to her husband, Billy's father, who left her
- is laughed at on the estate for having introduced so many 'uncles' into the family
- is hard up, slovenly in her dress and slapdash in her housekeeping
- is self-centred and concerned more with her own affairs than the welfare of her children.
- sets a bad example
- lacks motherly feelings

## Mrs Casper says

- 'Just you wait lad! Just you wait 'til tonight!' (4)
- 'And don't be still up when I come in.' (7)
- 'Talk sense, Billy, how can I hit him?' (24)
- 'Course I'm bothered. But it's only a bird. You can get another can't you?' (24)
- 'Billy! Come back here, you young bugger!' (24)

## Commentary

Mrs Casper, like Jud, is a 'flat' character: we see only one side of her personality. Having been unfaithful to her husband, she has been left to bring up the family on her own. She must find it hard to make ends meet, but she is a hurried and careless housekeeper and mother who makes no effort to create a comfortable and loving home for her sons. She expects Billy to light the fire, run errands and get his own tea. Mrs Casper appears in Episodes 4, 7, 24 and 25.

### Key point

**Barry Hines has said that if he were writing the novel now he would probably make Jud and Mrs Casper more sympathetic, and write more about them (Penguin Afterword). For example, Jud could be shown working underground in the mine, which might make us understand better how much the loss of £10 means to him. It would also make them more rounded characters.**

One thing Mrs Casper does devote time to is getting ready for her evenings out. The boyfriends she brings back late at night seem more significant in her life than Jud and Billy, to whom she shows very little affection apart from calling Billy 'love' sometimes. She is uninterested in Billy's personal life, only half listening to him and cutting short his account of converting the shed for Kes (7). Her refusal to buy him games clothes causes him to stand out painfully from the other boys (18). When Billy runs to her for physical comfort after Kes is killed, she pushes him away in embarrassment (24). Although she sympathises with his loss she has no idea how much Kes meant to him, and dares only rebuke Jud mildly.

Billy's tall story (15) shows how much Mrs Casper has failed him. Breakfast in bed might be a tall story for most teenagers, but a loving mother, comfortable surroundings and sufficient food would not be.

Mrs Casper has no control over Billy or Jud, and seems afraid of the latter. The only time she tries to exert some discipline is when she grumbles about noisy rows (7 and 24). It is not surprising that her sons are badly behaved, for she makes no attempt to set them an example. According to Jud, she frequently comes home drunk and often stays out all night (7). She asks Billy (who is only 15) for a cigarette and bribes him to be in bed before she gets home on Saturday night (7).

She swears, bribes, threatens and tries to use physical force when he refuses to go to the shops, although he would have to ask for extra credit and would be late for school, facing a beating (4).

# Mr Gryce

- is headmaster of the secondary modern school Billy attends
- is authoritarian and a bully
- is more concerned with small matters than large issues
- depends on fear, threats and use of the cane to maintain discipline, and never listens
- prefers punishment to encouragement

## Mr Gryce says

- 'MACDOWALL! I might have known it!' (11)
- 'Or I'll make you sing like you've never sung before.' (11)
- 'Fast asleep during the Lord's Prayer! I'll thrash you, you irreverent scoundrel!' (13)
- 'You know it all, you young people, you think you're so sophisticated with all your *gear* and your music.' (14)

## Commentary

Mr Gryce may seem like a caricature of a head teacher, but Barry Hines says he is partly based on an actual headmaster who caned a harmless messenger (Penguin Afterword). He appears in Episodes 11, 13, 14 and 22.

For Hines, Gryce represents all that was bad in 1960s education in secondary modern schools. More concerned with maintaining discipline than bringing out the best in his pupils, he is feared by boys and staff alike, though he is laughed at behind his back.

A tyrant and a bully, Gryce refuses to listen to explanations and expects the worst of everyone, as he does of MacDowall in assembly, for example. He is totally negative in his attitude, basing his daily routine on shouts, threats and regular beatings. He criticises the boys' joyless singing without perceiving the irony of his choice of hymn and Bible reading, with their emphasis on love and pastoral care. Sneering at young people's culture, he looks back to the good old days when pupils and parents accepted his authority without question (14), but does not realise that much of what he deplores in the school is the result of his own methods and approach to education. He also puts pressure on his staff, for instance when he insists that Mr Crossley singles out a particular boy for coughing in assembly (11).

Gryce's cruel streak is shown in his habit of making his victims wait for him after assembly (14). He carefully measures the distance of his cane from the boys'

hands, so that he can exert maximum force, having first lectured them on their worthlessness and declared his certainty that they will soon be back for more corporal punishment. He does not suggest ways in which they might improve, and he does not try to discover underlying causes of problems such as why Billy fell asleep in assembly. His unjust treatment of the messenger exposes his blindly domineering attitude.

Later in the day, Gryce is more concerned with trying to swipe Billy for missing his appointment than giving him encouragement before his important interview (22). His last action, cuffing a small boy on the head for walking on the wrong side of the corridor, illustrates his habit of focusing on trivial matters instead of wider issues.

# Mr Farthing

- teaches Billy English
- has a positive attitude to education
- instils good discipline, makes his lessons interesting, is popular and is respected by the boys
- despises bullies
- is a good listener
- has a sense of humour
- is interested in his pupils beyond school hours

## Mr Farthing says

- 'It all sounds very skilful and complicated, Billy.' (15)
- 'First one to find it gets a house point.' (15)
- 'Well, what's it like to be bullied? You don't like it much, do you?' (16)
- 'I don't know, you always seem to cop it, don't you, Casper?' (16)
- 'Marvellous, Casper! Brilliant! That's one of the most exciting things I've ever seen!' (20).

## Commentary

Most of the teachers in Billy's school are presented as uninspiring, fussy and often cruel. Farthing is a complete contrast. Barry Hines, who also taught English at one time, has said that there is a touch of himself in Farthing. He appears in Episodes 15, 16 and 20.

Farthing's interest in his pupils sets him apart from the other teachers. He asks Billy about his beating and later, seeing he is not listening, tries to draw him into the lesson (15). Billy's inability to think of a subject for his talk does prompt one outburst, when Mr Farthing accuses him of spoiling things for everyone and follows this with a threat of class punishment. But the boys respect him because he is fair, tries to make their lessons interesting and does not treat 4C as idiots (16).

Colin Welland as Mr Farthing in the film *Kes*

Farthing also uses incentives, like the house point for the first boy to find the meaning of 'fiction' in the dictionary (15). He has a relaxed relationship with his class but keeps good discipline. He knows how to make boys feel comfortable with him, and does not correct their grammar during their talks. When Billy joins him at the front of the class Farthing prompts him when necessary, interjecting words of encouragement or praise.

A good teacher, he uses Billy's talk as an opportunity to expand the vocabulary and understanding of everyone. Unlike many teachers, he is prepared to confess ignorance of a subject and to learn from a pupil.

Farthing despises bullies who attack weaker people, and this is why he gets angry with MacDowall after the fight (16) and shakes him 'like a terrier shakes a rat', to let him know what it feels like.

### Pause for thought

Do you think that Farthing is right to behave in this way? It was not against the law at the time of the novel, but could he have found a more positive way of dealing with MacDowall?

Unlike Mr Gryce, Farthing is prepared to listen. Talking to Billy after the fight (16) he waits patiently until he stops crying, draws him out and lets him confide in him in his own time. This is an important point in the novel, for we learn more about Billy here than almost anywhere else in the story. Farthing is sympathetic but realistic, asking Billy to think why he is so often in trouble, and also about his future. Unlike many teachers, he is objective about his own actions, agreeing that he treated Billy harshly for not concentrating after the beating. He shows his sense of humour when he laughs at Billy's impersonation of a stern teacher.

Finally, not only does Farthing know where Billy lives, but he also asks if he may watch Kes fly. He is captivated by what he sees (20). During that time he defers to Billy's expertise and does what he is told. Later he discusses the qualities of kestrels on equal terms with Billy. With more people like Farthing on the staff, Billy might have a better school record.

# Mr Sugden

* teaches games
* is self-important
* is obsessed with football
* is a sadistic bully

### Mr Sugden says

* 'I'd sooner take meat away from a starving lion than take the ball away from that thing.' (18)
* 'If he thinks I'm running my blood to water for ninety minutes, and then having the game deliberately thrown away at the last minute, he's another think coming!' (19)

### Commentary

Having studied physical education at Loughborough Training College and taught PE at one time, Barry Hines has probably met more than one fanatic like Sugden, who appears in Episodes 18 and 19.

Sugden is an absurd figure, first in his violet tracksuit embellished with a variety of badges and later in his number 9 Manchester United kit (18). In some ways he is pathetic. He is unaware that Tibbut is making fun of him when they discuss the difference between Manchester United and Liverpool kits, and while his main concern is to show off his football skills, the boys realise he is past it: 'He's like a chuffing carthorse' (18). They resent the way he takes first pick as captain and cheats to win, tugging opponents' clothes, giving goals and deciding penalties favouring his own team.

Obsessive about football, Sugden has no time for boys who are no good at, or do not like, organised games. He lets captains select their own teams, ensuring that weaker members of the class are left until last, and is quick to criticise the players. Perhaps he once hoped to play in the Football League; this might explain his use of club kits and switching between roles as commentator, Manchester United captain and authoritarian teacher.

**Pause for thought**

Although Sugden is a sadistic bully, is he also rather a pathetic figure, with his fantasy matches, immaculate Manchester United kit and his belief that he is a good footballer? Do you feel at all sorry for him?

Like Mr Gryce, Sugden has a vicious streak. He enjoys humiliating Billy, mocking him for not knowing the meaning of 'stimulating' (and then mis-spelling it out loud himself), making him wear outsize shorts, and swiping at him when they run on to the field (18). He also directs a slamming ball at Billy when he lets in an unsaveable goal: 'Slack work, lad. Slack work' (18). He is unsympathetic when Billy says he will miss his dinner, but has no chance to remonstrate when Billy deliberately lets in the winning goal and runs quickly off the pitch. Revenge is saved for later.

Sugden's swagger fades when a mongrel invades the field to play with the ball. Backing away, terrified, he sends Billy for cricket bats to drive it off, and gives no praise when Billy instead leads the dog away. Nor does he join the rest of the class in applauding Billy's impressive gymnastic landing from the crossbar. A better teacher would recognise Billy's potential as an athlete.

It is insensitive of Sugden to say that Billy looks as if he has taken Thalidomide. This was a drug given to pregnant women in the late 1950s and 1960s, which caused deformities (including loss or drastic shortening of limbs) in their babies.

Sugden's revenge for his team's defeat comes when Billy tries to avoid having a shower (19). Sending him back, he sadistically forces Billy to stand under the cold water jets. Deaf to appeals, in this brutal punishment he shows himself as perhaps even worse than Gryce.

# Minor characters

## Mr Crossley and the anonymous teacher

Mr Crossley teaches mathematics, and the anonymous teacher in Billy's maths class probably does so too. Neither seems closely involved with the pupils.

Mr Crossley is a caricature of a typical schoolmaster who lacks understanding of his charges. Quick to pounce on Billy, he is angry because his beautiful register has been spoilt and fussily tries to amend it (10). His sarcastic comments reflect

his displeasure. Flushing and panicking when instructed by Gryce to find the cougher in assembly, he chooses MacDowall at random (11).

The anonymous teacher, who may be sitting with the class or may teach them mathematics, reads while the boys work. He seems distanced, looking up occasionally to check on them. He does, however, suggest that Billy might like a glass of water after Jud peers through their classroom door (22).

## MacDowall

MacDowall is large for his age and a bully. He deserts Billy on the day of the bird-nesting expedition (5). Leader of the gang with whom Billy roamed the estate before he found Kes, he resents his defection.

With a reputation as a troublemaker, he is the obvious choice for Mr Crossley as a culprit for coughing (11). Mr Gryce makes this clear in his reaction.

MacDowall and Billy criticise each other's families while waiting to be beaten (14) and agree to settle their argument later. MacDowall then tries to intimidate Billy (16), insults his family, and suggests that Jud is not his 'right brother'. Fending off Billy's attack, he overpowers him, but receives a taste of his own medicine from Mr Farthing.

## Tibbut

Tibbut also fails to turn up for bird-nesting (5). Once Billy's friend and a member of the gang, he tells Mr Farthing that Billy never joins them because he is 'crackers' about his hawk. His bitter comment prompts Farthing to ask Billy to tell the class about Kes (15). Tibbut talks to Jud when he is searching the school, and later warns Billy that Mr Gryce has been looking for him (22).

## Mr Porter

Mr Porter, who employs Billy to do his newspaper round, is critical of everything he does. He disapproves of boys from the Valley Estate and constantly threatens to replace Billy with someone from a better area. Perhaps he can employ Billy more cheaply than another boy, but it may be that in spite of his prejudice he realises Billy needs the money. He smugly believes (wrongly) that Billy has never taken anything of his because he has never given him a chance. He appears in Episodes 2 and 3.

## The farmer

Concerned to protect his birds, the farmer is initially suspicious of Billy's motives when he wants to see the kestrels' nest. But, noting Billy's enthusiasm, he changes his mind, letting him come nearer, showing an interest in his ambition, and giving him useful information (5). They probably become friends, for Billy tells Mr Farthing of a farmer he knows who watches owls in his yard at night (20).

Mind map illustrating the interaction between characters in the novel

**Mrs Rose**
The betting officer. Tells Billy Jud's bet would have won him more than £10

**Valley Estate**
Includes disapproving neighbours, small boy on tricycle, the fishmonger and the butcher

**Farmer**
Owns the land where Billy sees the kestrel. Suggests he goes to the library for information

**Mr Porter**
The newsagent. Employs Billy, who steals from him. Grumpy and suspicious

**Youth employment officer**
Suggests mainly unsuitable work for Billy

**Milkman**
Offers Billy a ride, not knowing he has already stolen from him

**Mr Casper**
Does not appear in the novel. Took Billy to the cinema. Left home when he caught his wife being unfaithful

**Mrs Casper**
Mother of Jud and Billy. Unfaithful to her husband. Self-centred. An uncaring mother to her children

**Billy**
Central character in the novel. Son of Mrs and Mr Casper, who has left home. Probably a half-brother to Jud

**Librarian**
Refuses to lend Billy, or let him read, a book on falconry

**Jud**
Son of Mrs Casper. A bully. Kills Kes in revenge for losing the chance to win £10. Probably a half-brother of Billy

**Mr Gryce**
Head teacher. Runs school through fear and corporal punishment. Billy is one of his victims

**Mr Sugden**
Self-important PE teacher. Picks on Billy in games lesson and in showers

**Tibbut**
Lets Billy down over bird-nesting. Resents his defection from the gang. Suggests Kes as a subject for Billy's talk

**MacDowall**
Lets Billy down over bird-nesting. Resents his defection from the gang, which he leads. Fights Billy at break

**Other members of the school community**
The messenger, the smokers, Billy's classmates, a maths teacher

**Mr Farthing**
Teaches Billy English. Breaks up the fight. Listens to Billy's confidences. Comes to watch him flying Kes

**Mr Crossley**
Teaches maths. Fussy and sarcastic when Billy interrupts the register

## The librarian

The librarian's neat, methodical actions reflect her respect for order, and a narrow outlook. She is a contrast to the farmer, who is prepared to change his mind. Probably judging Billy by his address, and without the imagination to perceive his sense of urgency, she is not prepared to let him touch a book until he produces the regulation form. She appears in Episode 6.

## Mrs Rose

Mrs Rose shows no sympathy for Billy when he discovers that Jud's horses have won and Jud has lost money from the unplaced bet. Describing Jud's violence in the betting shop, she seems to relish the thought of his revenge on Billy. She represents the world of the estate and its casual acceptance of violence. Mrs Rose appears in Episode 24.

## The youth employment officer

We should, perhaps, have some sympathy with the youth employment officer, as Billy appears to be uninterested in his future, except for refusing to become a miner. Billy is probably preoccupied during their meeting, wondering how Jud will exact his revenge. However, the interviewer aggravates the situation by talking over Billy's head about apprenticeships and exams, even though Billy has made it clear that he has 'a job to read and write'. He is happy to release Billy when he asks to go. Like the librarian, his response to Billy is regulated by accepted norms of behaviour. He appears in Episode 23.

## The smokers

The three boys make the innocent messenger take the evidence of their smoking, and bare their teeth menacingly when he tries to explain this to Mr Gryce (14). Their beating does not prevent them gathering at break for another smoke in the cycle shed (16). They are another example of unchecked bullying in Billy's world.

## The messenger

The messenger cannot stand up to the older boys when they force their cigarettes, lighters and matches on him (14). Refused a hearing by Gryce, he is beaten with the others. Not knowing how to present his hand for the cane, he suffers most from the beating.

## Billy's father

Billy's father does not appear in the novel, but he has an important role. Billy's tall story and his flashback in the cinema reveal how much he misses his father, and how life has changed since he left on discovering his wife's infidelity. With his father at home, Billy might have developed very differently.

**Review your learning**

(Answers are given on page 81.)

1 Who says: 'I shouldn't like to think it were my job to learn you owt'?

2 Who says: 'He never knocks about wi' anybody else now, he just looks after this hawk all t'time'?

3 Why does Billy have to run his paper round?

4 What is Jud's reaction to Billy stealing *A Falconer's Handbook*?

5 Why does the farmer change his mind and let Billy approach the nest?

6 In what way is Mrs Casper a 'flat' character?

7 What does Mr Gryce think is wrong with the present generation of boys?

8 The messenger is an insignificant character who contributes little to the story. Why do you think Hines included him among the boys awaiting punishment?

9 With whom do your sympathies lie in the episode when Billy tries to borrow a book? Why?

# Themes

> What is a theme?
> What does it add to a novel?
> What are the main themes in this novel?
> How do they reflect Barry Hines's interests and attitudes?

A theme is an idea or train of thought running through a narrative, often connected to a particular vein of imagery. In a novel a theme provides a thread of continuity in the story, and quite often several related themes link together to form a pattern. In a sense, themes are what a novel is really about: the events and characters may be the subject on one level, but at a deeper level the novel is about a more general underlying idea such as love or loyalty.

In *A Kestrel for a Knave* there are major themes and minor themes, all of which help us to understand Billy as a person. The major themes are:

* the influence on Billy of four different environments: home, school, the Valley Estate, nature
* bullying

The minor themes are:

* animals
* imaginative games
* Billy's search for warmth (in a physical as well as an emotional sense)

Kes herself plays a thematic role as a symbol

## The environment

Billy's home, his school, the estate he lives on, and above all the country beyond play a major role in shaping his character.

### Billy's home environment

Billy is deprived of love, care and attention. His home is cold and bleak. Admittedly his mother is not well off and has no husband to support her, but she does not make any effort to provide a decent home life. She strews clothes around the house, runs out of basic foods, leaves dirty crockery in the kitchen and does not bother to draw the curtains in the morning. It is not surprising that before Billy has Kes he spends his spare time elsewhere on the estate.

Billy's longing for a more comfortable existence is revealed in his envious insight into comfortable middle-class life on Firs Hill, and in the warm, cosy, spotlessly clean shed where he spends his evenings with Kes.

Personally, Mrs Casper is slovenly. She wears skirts pinned together with safety pins, and does not provide adequate clothing for Billy. His windcheater has a broken zip, he tells Mr Sugden that he does not wear pants or a vest, and his pumps leak during the games lesson. When he strips in the shower room his skin is 'ingrained with ancient dirt'. This suggests that Mrs Casper does not concern herself with his personal hygiene.

Mrs Casper is lazy, and Billy probably feels resentful that he has to light the fire each morning before his paper round, do her chores and get his own tea. Her response to his refusal to go shopping is to swear at him and try to use force. If she has any affection for him she doesn't show it. She appears to have no respect, either for herself or for her sons, so it is not surprising that they have little respect for her.

### Pause for thought

It could be argued that at 15 Billy is too old to be told by his mother to wash properly. What do you think?

Totally self-centred, Mrs Casper goes out frequently in the evening, leaving Billy to come and go as he pleases. She gets drunk often and brings men home for the night. A more responsible parent might have prevented Billy joining MacDowall's gang of boys, who wander the estate, getting into trouble with the police.

### Pause for thought

Who do you think is a worse influence on Billy — Mrs Casper or Jud?

Billy may think he likes this lack of parental control, but most teenagers feel more secure when they are expected to conform to certain standards of behaviour. Billy needs someone to love — someone who loves him in return, is ready with comfort and sympathy, but is also prepared to take a firm line when necessary.

Unfortunately for Billy, Jud is not a brother he can look up to. He lacks moral integrity; for instance, he is not shocked by Billy's theft from the bookshop, only surprised that Billy took the risk for a mere book. He is a vindictive bully who sees violence as the answer to everything, whether he is forcing Billy to reveal the location of the kestrels' nest or reacting furiously in the betting shop when he discovers his bet has not been placed. He seems to have little respect for women — either his 'birds' or his mother. All in all, there is no one to set Billy an example.

The theme of Billy's home life is presented partly through the reactions of his neighbours, who are rather like the chorus in an Ancient Greek drama: they observe from a distance and occasionally comment on events, but take no part in

the action. They always appear at the end of an episode, as if to round off another chapter in the Casper family life.

At times they are invisible and remote presences, as when Mrs Casper grumbles at Jud and Billy for fighting in Episode 7: 'You're a couple o' noisy buggers, you two. I bet they can hear you at t'other side o' t'estate.' They come out to look when Billy takes Kes out on the estate in Episode 12, staring until Kes outstares them. In Episode 23 Billy, searching for Kes and Jud, suddenly jumps out in front of a woman who comments: 'Ee, what a family that is.'

Finally, the neighbours are drawn to their doorways and garden gates by the noise of the three-cornered fight between Billy, Mrs Casper and Jud in Episode 25. They watch as Billy bursts from the house, followed by his mother, who glances quickly at the audience. She remains outside long after Billy disappears, but even though it is raining the neighbours outstay her, this time saying nothing.

## The school environment

Ten of the 26 episodes in the novel are set at Billy's secondary school. It is an important part of his life, but its influence is almost totally discouraging. About to leave school, Billy regards himself as barely literate, with very limited prospects for employment other than down the mine.

### Key point

We know nothing of Billy's primary education, but his years at the secondary modern have clearly had a negative effect on him. Not having passed the 11+ exam, he would regard himself, and be regarded by others, as a failure. Promising pupils were siphoned off to grammar schools while the less academic majority went to secondary moderns, creating a divide between children in the same neighbourhood. (See 'Education in the 1960s' in the Context section.)

In the four years since Billy moved up into secondary school he has earned a reputation as stupid and troublesome. In Episode 16 he admits to Mr Farthing that he is occasionally 'a bad lad', but protests, 'I'm not that bad, I'm no worse than stacks o' kids, but they just seem to get away with it.' He feels that he gets 'into bother for nowt'. Most of us know of someone who gets a name as a troublemaker, and once acquired, this kind of reputation tends to stick. Incidents in the novel when Billy gets into trouble include falling asleep from exhaustion and not having the correct games kit — both problems that can ultimately be attributed to his defective home life.

Most of the staff at Billy's school follow Mr Gryce's example of maintaining discipline with fear, physical punishment and sarcasm, creating a hostile rather than a caring environment. Billy tells Mr Farthing in Episode 16 that, apart from him, the teachers cannot be bothered with 4C, the lowest stream in his year. They don't try to teach them anything, and keep looking at their watches. 'They're allus

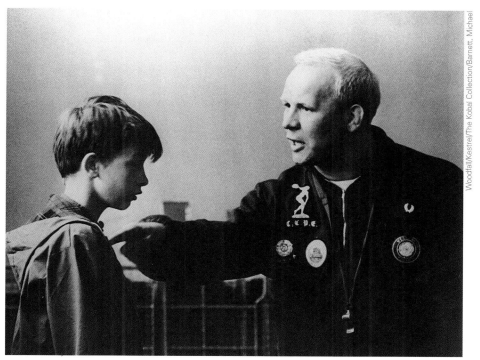

Woodfall/Kestrel/The Kobal Collection/Barnett, Michael

Billy is told off by Mr Sugden in the film *Kes*

callin' us idiots, an' numbskulls, an' cretins.' It does not seem to occur to the teachers that their pupils are as 'fed up wi' them' as they are with their pupils.

Billy's mathematics lesson is an example of unstimulating work set by an uninvolved teacher who sits at the front of the class reading a book. By contrast, in English lessons Farthing encourages, praises, listens and tailors his lessons to his pupils' abilities. As a result, the boys respond positively and respect him. He also shows an interest in their home lives and their plans for work when they leave school. Billy says Farthing is the only teacher he can really talk to.

We cannot imagine any boy wishing to discuss his problems with Gryce, whose constant fault-picking, reliance on the cane, refusal to listen and contempt for the younger generation expose him as a man out of his depth, though he would not recognise this. He harks back to the good old days of City Schools without facing the fact that if discipline in his school has regressed, the responsibility is mainly his.

Gryce's treatment of Billy in Episode 22, when he emerges after hiding from Jud, is typical. First batting Billy about the ears, Gryce comments disparagingly on his unsuitability for any employment. Pursuing him into an empty classroom, he tries unsuccessfully to follow up his words with further swipes, overbalancing in the attempt. Billy escapes and Gryce takes out his anger on a nearby boy.

While Mr Crossley is merely ineffectual, relying on sarcasm to keep the boys in place, Mr Sugden is a bully who uses physical as well as verbal means. Dismissive of anyone who fails to take games seriously, he regards his lessons as opportunities to show off his own prowess rather than to encourage boys to improve their skills. For instance, he does not associate Billy's natural agility with a possible aptitude for football, but instead sends Billy into goal, out of the way. His vindictive nature is particularly evident in Episode 19, when he forces Billy to stand under cold showers in revenge for Billy's deliberate failure to prevent the other side scoring a winning goal. While the rest of the class are amused by Sugden's earlier treatment of Billy in the changing room, they see this further cruelty as excessive. They protest that Billy will catch pneumonia, and when this has no effect they refuse to move when told to leave.

**Pause for thought**

Crossley and Sugden might be said to be caricatures of teachers, rather than convincing characters. What is your opinion?

The effect of a negative regime of this kind is to induce rebellion and an attitude of 'us and them', rather than collaboration towards a common purpose. Billy smokes, perhaps to show off to younger boys but also as a kind of mute protest. Bullying and fights are part of school life, and reflect the school's domineering and brutal culture. Only Farthing tries to instil a more civilised ethos, teaching MacDowall that he should respect his fellow pupils, especially those who are weaker and smaller.

It is difficult to estimate how different Billy might have been in another, better school. Perhaps he would still lie to avoid punishment (as he does to Sugden and Gryce), and perhaps he would still be impertinent, as when he pretends to be deaf after his cuff over the ears in Episode 22. However, his truthful and respectful behaviour with Farthing suggests that he would respond positively to other good teachers too.

**Pause for thought**

To what extent do you think that well-maintained school buildings and grounds affect pupils' behaviour and attitudes?

The run-down and neglected physical environment of the school reflects the overall uncaring attitude. In Episode 17 Hines vividly describes the toilets, with the wet floor, whining cistern, overflowing waste bin and paper towels 'stuck to the tiles like transfers'. The floors of the changing room and corridor show wear and tear, and windows in classrooms are tightly shut, producing a stale and sweaty atmosphere.

Outside, the unwelcoming yard is windswept, with boys huddling in sheltered corners. Smokers lurk in the bike shed, and the coke pile is a perfect source of missiles.

For Billy, leaving school is not a jumping-off point, but a continuation of doing something he does not like. There has been no preparation at school or home for his youth employment interview. As a result, Billy has little self-respect (except for his success with Kes) and limited self-confidence. He admits in Episode 16: 'I'm not bothered. Owt'll do me'.

Like many other boys of his age at the time, Billy has been sadly let down by his school, which has branded him a slow learner and has focused on what he can't do rather than what he can. A more enlightened school would recognise his merits — his athleticism, his understanding of the natural environment, and the determination that enables him to learn about falconry and to train a kestrel — and might suggest, for instance, that he explore opportunities for an outdoor life working with animals.

## The urban environment

Valley Estate lies between the City and the countryside. They are linked by City Road where Mr Porter's shop, the library and the Palace Cinema are situated. It is one of many housing estates built soon after the Second World War that quickly became run down, demoralising the residents and leading to neglect and vandalism.

The mine lies between Valley Estate and the City, and is the likely future workplace of most of the less able boys leaving Billy's school. It does not offer an inviting prospect, since life down the pit is tough, exhausting and grimy. For Billy, who is not strong and loves the open air, the prospect of working under-ground all day is hateful.

### Text focus

Read from the beginning of Episode 26, 'Billy looked over his shoulder', until 'turned back, and stood before it' at the end of the paragraph before 'THE PALACE'.

➤ Try to visualise the appearance of the estate and the City Road, and their overall layout.

➤ Note that Barry Hines gives a detailed description of the squalid estate, to highlight the immediate background of Billy's life. He does not explicitly state its influence on Billy's development, but this is implicit in the unfavourable contrast with earlier descriptions of the natural environment.

● The sentences in this passage are very short. Why do you think this is?

● Compare this passage with the description of the urban environment from Firs Hill in Episode 2. What is the impact of these different views on the reader?

- Billy tells Mr Farthing in Episode 16 that he does not go to the school's evening youth clubs because he does not like organised games. In the past he and his friends sometimes went to the City, to the cinema or a coffee bar. Otherwise they went around the estate breaking into places and stealing, 'just for a bit of excitement'. Is the estate in any way to blame for their behaviour?
- Now that Billy no longer goes out with the gang, how does he spend his evenings?
- What evidence is there in the novel that Billy's former friends resent his leaving the gang?
- What more do we learn about the estate from the description of the surroundings of the betting shop in Episode 21?
- Think about how you would respond to living on the estate.

## The natural environment

Billy's estate lies between two distinct areas. It is quite close to the city, but it is also on the brink of the countryside, where he spends his happiest days. The fields and woods within a stone's throw of Billy's house provide an escape from the streets to surroundings where he is positive and self-confident.

### Pause for thought

Compare the differences in descriptive writing about the natural environment in Episodes 5 and 9 with that about the estate in Episodes 21 and 26. Since Hines shows Billy's world through his eyes, it is reasonable to assume that Billy hates the dilapidated estate, even though he has contributed to vandalising it in the past.

Billy tells Mr Farthing in Episode 20 how, when he was young, he used to go up on the cliffs in Scarborough to watch seagulls with his father. He must have spent a lot of time since then in the nearby country, for he is observant, naturally curious and knowledgeable about wildlife. Going bird-nesting in Episode 5, he examines a blade of grass and a scrap of moss. He observes the sleepy cows, the covey of partridges and the chattering blackbird, and listens to different types of birdsong. When he high-steps through brambles, he takes care to replace their protective cover over a nest of young thrushes. However, he also enjoys the physical release offered by nature, as when he climbs a tree or thrashes down undergrowth.

Billy's first sight of the female kestrel is a significant moment. When she emerges from her nest he knows instinctively how to behave; he kneels without moving, and when she looks away he eases himself gently into the hedge bottom to avoid disturbing her.

Nothing Billy has seen before has prepared him for the beauty of the male kestrel in flight. Through his eyes we watch its hovering and breathtaking use of air currents, its sudden stoop on its quarry, and its transfer of prey to its mate. Billy's ambition to have his own kestrel to train is partly realised by the help of the farmer who lets him come near the nest, questions him about his motives and offers him good advice. It is no coincidence that Billy's meetings with him and with Mr Farthing in the lunch break in Episode 20 take place in the open air, where Billy is most at ease. On each occasion he is treated without condescension as a person in his own right.

Billy seems equally relaxed in the country at night when he goes to collect Kes from Monastery Farm in Episode 9. He notices the texture of the air, the silver sheen reflected from the moon, and the curtain of trees above him stretching up to the stars. He practises and perfects a tawny owl's cry, and exchanges calls.

Billy's more positive attitude to his leisure hours after this event stems directly from Kes and, through her, the natural environment. He undertakes the daunting task of reading a whole falconry book, and then spends long hours training Kes, mostly outdoors. He abandons the gang and no longer gets into trouble with the police.

**Pause for thought**

How is Billy's pride in training Kes reflected in his talk to the class in Episode 15?

This new life does not mean that Billy undergoes a sudden, dramatic change in character. He still steals, swears, lies and smokes, but he has found something he can do well. His sense of achievement gives him a new pride. 'It's trained. I've trained it,' he tells the boy with the tricycle in Episode 12.

There is still much for Billy to learn, and he spends long hours perfecting Kes's training to the lure. The reference to his farmer friend in Episode 20 suggests that he sometimes visits him to share experiences.

When Kes disappears, Billy ventures into the countryside at dusk to look for her. While his night-time excursion in Episode 9 is lit by the moon, this journey in Episode 24 is different. The charcoal sky and failing light seem to echo the darkness of Billy's fears and he makes slow progress in the slashing rain. Stumbling and falling, and unable to see clearly, he loses his way but perseveres until he reaches Monastery Farm. His journey is fruitless, for there is no wall, no nest and no Kes.

**Pause for thought**

'Billy stared over the hedge across at the farm for a long time. Then he started to shiver and turned away, and slowly made his way back through the woods.' Billy is soaked through and cold, but is there another reason for his shiver?

Billy will probably find solace for Kes's loss in the open air, and perhaps one day he will train the goshawk he mentions to Mr Farthing.

# Bullying

Although bullying is a factor in Billy's home and school environment, it is also a theme in its own right. Here are some reminders of different forms of bullying for you to follow up. Remember that bullying can be mental, verbal or physical.

- Mr Porter: Episode 2
- Mrs Casper: Episode 4
- Jud: Episodes 1, 7, 24, 25
- Mr Gryce: Episodes 11, 13, 14, 22
- the smokers: Episode 14
- MacDowall: Episodes 14 and 16
- Billy's class: Episodes 10 and 15 (later, after his talk, they show more sympathy for his problems)
- Mr Sugden: Episodes 18 and 19

# Animals

This theme is closely linked with that of the natural environment. Except for the dog, all the animals seen by Billy are beyond the estate, either nearby or on Firs Hill on the edge of the moor.

The story is almost as much about Kes as about Billy, but the other animals have a thematic role rather than a function in the plot. Most of them are mentioned briefly in the context of Billy's ramblings in the country. They bring the scenes to life and demonstrate the diversity of wildlife in the natural environment, which is an unknown world to most residents of the estate. Billy's closeness to animal life is evident when he tells Mr Farthing that before getting Kes he reared a fox cub and several birds including magpies, jackdaws and a jay. His account of training Kes in Episode 15, the description of him flying her, and his conversation with Mr Farthing in Episode 20 all give us a deeper insight into the skill involved in handling Kes.

Jud's assumption that hawks are a menace to farmers ('They eat all their poultry an' everything', Episode 7) reflects

## Pause for thought

After watching Billy fly Kes in Episode 20, Farthing asks him why she is more special than animals he has kept before. Billy replies: 'I don't know right. It just is that's all.' Pressed to find an answer, he shrugs his shoulders. Why do you think he finds it so difficult to express his feelings about her?

## Key point

Animals mentioned in the novel include worms, tadpoles, cows, a dog, fox cubs and 16 species of bird (not including those listed in the epigraph). Watch out for these as you read, and make a list of the episodes where they appear.

his urban outlook. Habitually violent, his reaction to hearing about Kes is to threaten to shoot her.

The incident of the dog on the football pitch in Episode 18 is intended partly to show up Mr Sugden, but it is also another example of Billy's good relationship with animals.

# Imaginative games

Billy never invents games in the natural environment, where he has better things to do, but in the man-made environment of his home, the estate and the school he amuses himself with games ranging from making a snowstorm in an orange bottle, to blowing bubbles or pretending to be animals. Perhaps they are a diversion from everyday monotony; perhaps they compensate for his lack of friends; perhaps they are simply the creations of an imaginative mind.

## Pause for thought

**Billy plays imaginative games in Episodes 2, 17, 18, 20 and 23. Identify them and make notes to keep for your revision.**

# Warmth

Billy is someone who feels the cold, both literally and metaphorically. Small and skinny, he frequently tries to warm himself physically. He also needs emotional warmth in his family relationships and at school, but does not receive it except from Mr Farthing.

## Key point

**We see Billy seeking some kind of warmth:**

* at home: Episodes 1, 2, 4, 24,
* on his paper round: Episode 2
* at school: Episodes 15 (in his tall story), 16, 17, 18, 19, 22
* in the cinema: Episode 26.

# Kes

Kes is a major presence throughout the novel, both as an actor in the plot and as a symbol of Billy's individuality and independent spirit. Both Kes and Billy resist being tamed. As Hines says in his Afterword to the Penguin Classics edition, Billy is 'a survivor, a tough little character'; he is unwittingly describing his own indomitable attitude to life when he explains to Mr Farthing in Episode 20: 'it's not a pet, Sir, hawks are not pets…it's trained that's all. It's fierce, an' its wild, an' it's not bothered about anything, not even me right.'

With Kes waiting for him at home, dependent on him in some ways but also free in spirit, Billy has a purpose in life and keeps out of trouble on the estate. With her death he loses this focus and the only thing he loves. We cannot be sure how he will react after his initial grief, but we hope that his own free spirit will not be dimmed for long.

**Review your learning**

(Answers are given on page 82.)

1 What is a theme in a novel?

2 What are the major themes in *A Kestrel for a Knave*?

3 In what way is Kes a symbol?

4 Using your list of Billy's imaginative games (Pause for thought, page 55), think about whether they stem from creativity or boredom, or both. Try to analyse your reasons.

5 Why do you think Barry Hines puts so much emphasis on Billy's search for warmth?

6 How much can you remember of the description of the view from Firs Hill in Episode 2? Reread it if necessary. In what ways do Episodes 21 and 26 provide a clearer picture of Billy's more immediate environment?

7 Using Episodes 2 and 26, draw a plan of Billy's world and its landmarks.

# Style

➢ What is style in literature?
➢ What are the main features of Barry Hines's style in this novel?
➢ From whose points of view do we learn about Billy and his environment?
➢ What is the setting and how does it influence the atmosphere?
➢ What part does descriptive language play in the novel?
➢ How is language used to portray character?

Jonathan Swift, the eighteenth-century author of *Gulliver's Travels*, defined style as 'proper words in proper places'. He meant that authors aim to use the most appropriate diction (words) and syntax (the order of words in sentences), according to the context in which they are writing, to express meaning and mood.

Style can be formal, as in serious newspaper articles and textbooks. It can be informal, with a more relaxed tone, and may include colloquial language when the aim is to portray ordinary life realistically. Much writing uses a mixture of formal and informal styles.

Barry Hines uses this novel for social commentary on education and life on urban housing estates in the 1960s. The language in the main narrative is quite formal and mainly Standard English, but much of the dialogue is colloquial and in regional dialect, and some of the characters use slang and swear words. Hines is a master of economical language, creating a variety of effects with a precise choice of diction. Scenes conveying gritty realism alternate with striking imagery, descriptive writing of great beauty, and lively or humorous passages.

## Viewpoint

The story is told by a third-person narrator (who refers to Billy by name or as 'he' or 'him') but we see the world through Billy's eyes.

The narrator in *A Kestrel for a Knave* is an onlooker and is uninvolved in events. The tone is unsentimental, even at the end when Billy has lost everything he cares for. In spite of this neutral tone and the absence of explicit comment on events, the narrative is not a cold account of what happens, because we are offered insights into Billy's inner feelings and thoughts. This is achieved mainly through his conversations with Mr Farthing, the flashbacks and his tall story.

**Key point**

Contrast this style with novels using a first-person narrator — an 'I' who is involved in the story. Examples include *To Kill a Mockingbird* by Harper Lee, *Jane Eyre* by Charlotte Brontë and *The Chrysalids* by John Wyndham.

Note how much we learn about Billy's basic level of literacy from his tall story in Episode 15, which Hines presents exactly as Billy writes it, rather than in Standard English.

# Setting and atmosphere

The novel is set in an area of about 10 square kilometres in South Yorkshire. From the edge of the town (called the City) it stretches towards the country along City Road. The estate lies on one side, with Billy's immediate area of countryside and Monastery Farm beyond. Mr Porter's shop and the cinema are on the other side of City Road, with Firs Hill branching off to the moor. The mine lies between the City and the estate. Billy's school is on the estate.

As we saw in the Themes chapter, all these places affect Billy's actions in some way on the day covered by the novel, and taken together they make up the geographical setting and atmosphere that have formed him.

The story is set in the 1960s (the novel was first published in 1968), by which time some of the buildings hastily erected in the years following the Second World War were showing the effects of poor design and shoddy construction. Valley Estate is one example, with its identical rows of houses, derelict gardens and scruffy open spaces.

The 1960s was the decade of the Beatles, the first British group to challenge US superiority in rock and roll, who dominated popular culture. Mr Gryce's sarcastic comment on 'music and *gear*' in Episode 14 is probably directed at young people infected with Beatlemania.

This was a time when class barriers were breaking down and writers were challenging established social norms and structures. John Osborne's 1956 play *Look Back in Anger* is an early example of this trend, and Alan Sillitoe's 1959 novel *The Loneliness of the Long Distance Runner* is another. Barry Hines's focus on run-down estates and inadequate schools follows the same pattern.

## Text focus

Read the first episode in the novel very carefully, noting how Barry Hines establishes the scene and atmosphere.
- The opening paragraph focuses on Billy and Jud's bedroom. Reading this description is rather like looking at a picture of a night scene in an art gallery. The first short negative statement sets the tone, and three more brief sentences build on our first impression. The window is a 'hard edged block' showing the night sky, and the darkness is gritty. The single-word sentence 'Silence', concluding the paragraph, emphasises the stillness.

➤ The second paragraph brings the picture to life, with movement and sound (Jud's snort and Billy's whimper) suggesting restless sleep. Note how Billy seems to be trying to edge towards the outside of the bed, away from Jud, even though it is colder there; this reflects Billy's dislike of Jud.

➤ The third paragraph, with its detailed sequence of movement and sounds, stresses first the chill and discomfort of the shared bed and then the brutal awakening when the alarm goes off.

➤ Note that there is no physical description of Billy and Jud. We learn about them from what they say and do, and how they react to each other. From his first words Jud is revealed as cruel and abusive. Billy seems unable to retaliate.

➤ We are not told where the story is set, but the brothers use the South Yorkshire dialect. Many of the words are different from their equivalents in Standard English (for example, 'thi sen' for 'yourself') but their meaning is usually clear or easy to work out even for readers who are not from the same region.

➤ The dialogue between Jud and Billy consists of short sentences that come straight to the point. We are not told who is speaking, as it is obvious from the context.

◉ What evidence is there in the episode that Billy is younger than Jud?

◉ Might he have more than one reason for urging Jud to get up?

◉ Which words suggest movement?

◉ Besides the dialogue, Hines includes several words and phrases suggesting sound. Make a list of them. Why are they effective in this particular context?

◉ Billy's search for warmth is a minor theme in the novel. How is it established in the opening episode?

# Descriptive language

Barry Hines's art in reproducing a scene vividly stems from a keen eye for detail, precise diction and, to a large extent, imagery.

## Imagery

Imagery (the creation of mental images) is a key tool for a descriptive writer. It can take many forms, but metaphors and similes are the most common. Hines uses few metaphors, but his similes are distinctive features of the novel.

**Metaphors** compare two things by stating that one thing *is* another:

◉ 'Then the monster [Jud] began to rumble' (Episode 8).

**Similes** make direct comparisons, usually introduced by the words *like* or *as*. Here are three examples of similes in the novel. Read them carefully, trying to visualise what Hines is describing in each case:

◉ 'Then a speck appeared on the horizon. It [the kestrel] held like a star, then fell and faded' (Episode 5).

- 'For most of the game most of the boys had been as fixed as buttons on a pinball machine' (Episode 18).
- Billy, standing on the stile looking for Kes: '…he straightened up, balancing like the top man of a pyramid of tumblers' (Episode 24).

As you work through the novel, make a list of other similes that you enjoy. Keep them for your revision.

## Other techniques

Hines also employs techniques other than imagery in his descriptive writing.

**Short sentences**, or sentences broken frequently by commas, is a common technique.

- 'Slowly. Hand. Foot. Hand. Foot. Never stretching, never jerking. Always compact, always balanced. Sometimes crabbing to by-pass gaps in the stonework, sometimes back-tracking several moves to explore a new line; but steadily meandering upwards, making for the highest window' (Episode 9). Here the style creates a vivid impression of steady, slow movement.
- 'The first stroke made him cry. The second made him sick' (Episode 14). Further comment would dilute the fierceness of the boy's pain.
- 'The shed door was open. The hawk was gone' (Episode 23). The brief, stark sentences, with no elaboration, stress the agony of the moment.
- 'He <u>started</u> to run. He reached the stile leading into the woods and <u>ran</u> over it, <u>dragging</u> the lure behind him. It <u>caught</u> on the cross-bar and <u>jerked</u> him to a halt. He <u>tugged</u> it, wound the cord round his hand and <u>rushed</u> forward' (Episode 24). Note the strong, active verbs — underlined here — evoking the impetus of Billy's desperate dash.

**Long sentences** are also effective.

- 'The estate was teeming with children: tots hand in hand with their mothers, tots on their own, and with other tots, groups of tots and Primary School children; Secondary School children, on their own, in pairs and in threes, in gangs and on bikes. Walking silently, walking on walls, walking and talking, quietly, loudly, laughing; running, chasing, playing, swearing, smoking, ringing bells and calling names: all on their way to school' (Episode 4).

Look at the way punctuation is used in these two sentences, and the effect of repetition. In the second sentence, Hines breaks the general rule of including a main (finite) verb in every sentence. Think about why he does this here.

Frequent references to **colour**, and different degrees of darkness and light, enrich Hines's word pictures. Here are four brief examples for you to look at. Watch out for others and make a note of them:

- the colours in the early morning sky, as Billy leaves the dark house to collect the newspapers; the street lamps and lighted windows (Episode 2)

- the brilliance of the early morning when Billy goes bird-nesting, complemented by the splashes of flowers in the fields (Episode 5)
- hymn books contrasting with the colours of the boys' clothes (Episode 11)
- Tibbut scrutinising the brightly coloured games clothes of his team before deciding to be Spurs (Episode 18)

**Key point**

Hines also uses colour as a symbol of Billy's rising and falling fortunes. The fateful day starts as 'a hard-edged block the colour of the night sky' (Episode 1) and the weather remains gloomy all day. At break, the yard reflects 'the shifting grey and black of the low sky' (Episode 16). In the maths lesson, while Jud is on his way to find Billy at school, the sky is darkening. The curtained windows make the house dark when Billy enters, calling out for Jud. As he starts his search for Kes, the sky is charcoal, and it turns to black as he roams the fields and wood. He runs out into the dark night when he learns the truth, and fumbles his way through impenetrable blackness in the cinema. He buries Kes under the night sky, and goes to his dark room to bed.

In contrast, in the first flashback a brilliant day is dawning when Billy goes bird-nesting (Episode 5). The morning light comes in 'as clean as water'. Walking through the fields, he watches the sun rise, 'burning the cloud golden'. He falls asleep in its warmth before waking to see the kestrel. Similarly, the light from the moon on his night walk to Monastery Farm 'penetrated and lit the way' (Episode 9). His time with Kes is, for Billy, a golden time.

**Sound** adds a further dimension to descriptive passages. For example:
- the tinkling bell in Mr Porter's shop (Episode 2); the word 'tinkled' is an example of onomatopoeia — a word that sounds like its meaning
- the multitude of sounds in the playground (Episode 16)
- a car revving, moving off and fading away (Episode 20)

**Humour** enlivens Hines's prose through occasional wry observations:
- Mr Crossley's total absorption in trying to correct his register (Episode 10)
- Mr Gryce 'straining over the top of the lectern like a bulldog up on its hind legs' (Episode 11)
- Mr Sugden in his sports kit (Episode 18)

**Unsentimental and down-to-earth description** is a further feature of Barry Hines's style:

* the detailed description of Kes dismembering the sparrow, dragging out the intestines before she 'snuffled and gobbled them down' (Episode 20)
* Billy's discovery of Kes in the bin (Episode 24)
* the two final unemotional paragraphs of the book describing Billy's return home (Episode 26).

## Extracts for close examination

The extracts listed below are some of the best examples of Hines's descriptive writing in the novel.

* Billy's bird-nesting expedition, from 'The sun was up and the cloud band in the East' to 'a wide circle back to the telegraph pole' (Episode 5).
* Billy's journey to take a kestrel (the whole of Episode 9).
* Anderson's tale of the tadpoles (Episode 15). Note Anderson's fluent, realistic description, much of it in dialect.
* Billy's tall story (Episode 15). His expression, spelling and punctuation reveal his poor education as well as his inner feelings.
* The fight, from 'Billy ran at him' to 'Mr Farthing looked round at them, blazing' (Episode 16).
* Billy in the toilets (the whole of Episode 17).
* Billy's search for Kes from 'At first the handkerchief twirled and dipped' to 'started to run back across the fields towards the estate' (Episode 24).
* Billy finding Kes in the bin, from 'Billy broke from between them, out through the kitchen' to 'jesses dangling, its claws hooks in the air' (the end of Episode 24 and the start of Episode 25).
* The estate, from 'Billy looked over his shoulder' to 'daytime reference points about the maze of the estate' (Episode 26).
* Billy in the cinema, from 'THE PALACE' to 'No contact! No contact!' (Episode 26). Notice the way in which the author represents the images rushing through Billy's mind. This is called 'stream of consciousness'.

# Dialogue

Unlike many authors, Barry Hines never states directly who is speaking, although sometimes the preceding sentence makes it clear. For example:

> Mr Sugden studied his watch, as the ball was returned to him at the centre spot.

> 'Right then, the next goal's the winner!' (Episode 18)

Local inhabitants in *A Kestrel for a Knave* use the South Yorkshire dialect; the teachers speak Standard English. Short speeches are often used to reflect mood and situation, such as sleepiness at the start of Episode 1, and aggression by the time Jud is fully awake. Most of the bitter exchanges throughout the novel are short and to the point, and the language is often crude.

**Key point**

Barry Hines rarely describes how people speak, but the tone is usually obvious from their diction. There is never any confusion in the readers' mind. This is an effective way of achieving crisp and realistic speech.

Most other authors provide far more detail, stating who is talking, and often the tone of voice used. For example, John Wyndham in *The Chrysalids* writes: '"It's not S it's Z," Petra insisted fearfully,' and '"You mean it's a secret?" I asked, puzzled.'

Look at some other novels and examine different methods of reporting speech.

**Pause for thought**

Barry Hines has said that if he were writing the novel today he would not use dialect. 'It can be irritating to the reader and whatever methods you try, you don't capture the voice on the page. I think the best solution is to use dialect words to give the flavour of the region, but trying to reproduce northern working-class speech with the glottal stops as in "Goin' to t'cinema" doesn't work at all' (Penguin Afterword).

Do you think that the novel would be as effective with just the occasional dialect word? Or do you feel that dialect is fundamental to Hines's creation of place and atmosphere?

Most people in the novel have distinctive styles of speaking that reflect their characters. Jud, Mr Porter, Mr Gryce, Mr Sugden and MacDowall reveal their natural aggression in almost everything they say. Mrs Casper is less predictable. For example, in Episode 4 she moves smoothly from persuasive to abusive to threatening when she tries to make Billy do her shopping. Mr Farthing is a more rounded character, and this is shown in the different ways he speaks to his class, to Billy and to MacDowall.

Billy's language is much more varied, reflecting the different facets of his personality. Although he often uses dialect with short sentences, when he is relaxed and confident he speaks more fluently, with no trace of dialect.

**Review your learning**

(Answers are given on page 82.)

1  In what way is the narrator's tone of voice neutral?

2  What is the difference between the way Mr Farthing talks and Billy's usual way of speaking?

3  In which decade, and where, is the novel set?

4  In what ways does Hines use his novel as a vehicle for social comment?

5  To which group is Mr Gryce probably referring when he criticises popular music?

6  What is the difference between a simile and a metaphor?

7  In what way is Hines's dialogue different from that of many other novelists?

8  To what extent does the imagery in the novel contribute to our understanding of Billy's personality?

9  Make brief notes commenting on the following extract in the light of what you have learned about Hines's style:

12.20 p.m. Billy jump, jump, jumped on the line. 'Score, for Christ's sake somebody score.' Tick tick tick tick. Sugden missed again. He's blind, he's bleedin' blind. Sugden was crimson and sweating like a drayhorse, and boys began to accelerate smoothly past him, well clear of his scything legs and shirt-grabbing fists. (Episode 18)

# Tackling the exam

➤ What kinds of question are set in the exam?
➤ How should you plan your answers?
➤ How should you start and end essays?
➤ How should you use quotations and other evidence?
➤ What do you have to do to get an A*?

## Higher and foundation tiers

### Higher tier

Some higher-tier questions give brief directions, but others offer no guidance, expecting candidates to decide for themselves what to cover and how. For example:

1  **Choose two episodes in the novel you find dramatic. Write about:**
   * **what you think makes them dramatic**
   * **how the author makes them seem dramatic.**
2  **Do you think Billy has only himself to blame for what happens to Kes?**
3  **In what ways is the author's concern with social issues reflected in the novel?**
4  **What significant contributions does Kes make to the novel?**
5  **Choose three characters apart from Billy with whom you sympathise at some point in the novel. Show how the author invites your sympathy.**
6  **In what ways is humour used in the novel, and for what purpose?**

### Foundation tier

Foundation-tier questions usually give guidelines for planning and structuring answers, in the form of bullet points. For example:

1  **What is the importance of Mr Farthing in the novel? Write about:**
   * **how the author uses Mr Farthing in his commentary on the education system at that time**

  * **his teaching methods**
  * **his relationship with the boys**
  * **his readiness to listen**
  * **his attitude to bullying**
  * **his relationship with Billy**
2 **In what ways is Billy influenced by his environment? Write about:**
  * **Billy's home environment**
  * **his school environment**
  * **the Valley Estate**
  * **the nearby countryside**
3 **Which sequence of events in the novel do you find most memorable, and why? Write about:**
  * **what happens**
  * **how the author makes it memorable**
  * **your reasons for choosing the sequence**

# Answering the questions

Here are some hints on tackling exam questions:
* Read the directions printed on the first page of the paper.
* Make sure you know exactly what you have to do.
* Check how long you are advised to spend on writing your answer.
* Do not be tempted to run over time.
* Don't just retell the story. Demonstrate your appreciation of how the story is written, not just what happens in it.
* Be selective. Include what is most relevant to your answer.
* Remember that there is no right or wrong answer in GCSE English literature. If your references to the text are accurate, and you can support your views, the examiners will accept your argument as a personal response even if it does not accord with their own interpretation.
* Use formal English, with no colloquialisms.
* Ensure you spell literary terms, characters' names, places and the author's name correctly.
* Leave a few minutes at the end to check your answer for accuracy.

There are three main types of question in the GCSE exam. These focus on plot, character and theme. Here are some typical questions:

**In what ways do the flashbacks contribute to the story of Billy Casper?**

This question focuses on what happens and when, and how the flashbacks fit into the structure of the novel.

**Billy is a liar, a thief and a rebel, but he still engages our sympathy. Why do you think this is so?**

This question is based on the author's presentation of a character, and your personal response to that character.

**How is the theme of bullying presented in the novel?**

Here you are asked to analyse and discuss the importance of a major theme.

# Planning your answers

Spend a few minutes planning your essay before starting to write. Here are some suggestions:

* Read the question at least twice, making sure you understand the task.
* Highlight or underline key words or phrases.
* If your question has no bullet-point directions, consider what the examiners might have chosen if they had included them.
* Make a plan using bullet-point notes or a spider diagram (with the main key word in a circle in the middle and different strands of the essay emerging from the centre like a spider's web). If you use bulleted notes, leave a line between each one for second thoughts.
* Make sure your plan gives sufficient weight to each key word or phrase in the question.
* Keep your notes legible. If you run out of time you can refer the examiner to your plan.
* Before you start to write, check that you have covered the main issues and that everything is relevant to the question.

**Pause for thought**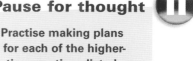

Practise making plans for each of the higher-tier questions listed on page 65. This is a useful exercise even if you are aiming for the foundation tier.

Experiment with different sorts of plan and decide what works for you. Some people like diagrammatic plans. Alternatively, make a list and number the points. Below is a plan for the following question.

**How is the theme of bullying presented in the novel?**

**1** Introduction. B a natural target for bullying. Give reasons.
**2** Theme of bullying runs throughout — even at the newsagent. At home — Mrs C. sometimes. Jud usually — physical and mental — undermining B's self-confidence.
**3** Jud rampaging through the school. Later, at home.
**4** Integral part of school life and important to author's portrayal of sec. mod. system. Insecure and disillusioned teachers. Sarcasm. Gryce bullies staff and boys. Sadistic Sugden.

5   Boys follow trend. B often mocked by boys. MacDowall. Farthing's attitude to bullying — contrast.

6   Conclusion. Bullying partly responsible for B's development and attitude to life. Could have been different with father at home?

# Starting your essay

Your introduction can be quite short, and can be presented in a number of ways. For example:

* one or two general but relevant comments on the topic
* how you interpret the question
* a brief summary of what you intend to say

*Do not* copy out the question on the exam paper. This wastes time and gains you no marks.

Below are three possible introductions for an answer to the following question.

**In what ways do the flashbacks contribute to the story of Billy Casper?**

**Introduction 1**
At the time that Barry Hines wrote the novel, flashbacks to the past were becoming popular in cinema and television. They were seen as a useful way of extending the span of the main narrative.

**Introduction 2**
Considering the contribution of flashbacks in *A Kestrel for a Knave* requires an analysis of their function, as well as an examination of what the novel would lack without them.

**Introduction 3**
Nearly five-sixths of the novel describes the events in this single day of Billy Casper's life. The flashbacks are therefore a small proportion of the whole. They are, however, a vital part of the structure.

# Ending your essay

Your conclusion can take several forms, such as:

* a summary of the argument
* a general comment on the topic
* a completely new idea, relevant to the topic

Below are three possible conclusions to the following question.

**In what ways do the flashbacks contribute to the story of Billy Casper?**

**Conclusion 1**

Each flashback gives us a different view of Billy: his early childhood memories; his first sighting of the kestrels; the night visit to Monastery Farm; his search for a book; his standing up to Jud's bullying, and taking Kes on to the estate during her training. Each contributes another different aspect of the rounded picture Barry Hines presents.

**Conclusion 2**

Billy's past to some extent determines the person he has become at 15. It is for this reason that the final flashback in the cinema is so important. Once, it seems, Billy lived in a secure world. We get a glimpse of what might have been.

**Conclusion 3**

Without these flashbacks we would have a narrower view of Billy, and none of his past. There would be no description of Billy's precious time with his father, of his first sight of the kestrels, or his night journey to the nest. Nor would we share an early stage in Kes's training. The novel would lose much of its interest.

# Using evidence

Examiners expect you to provide evidence to reinforce what you say in your answer. This can be in the form of short quotations or close reference to the text.

## Quotations

A good answer will include up to ten quotations. Here are some guidelines:
* Choose a variety of quotations to reveal your understanding and knowledge.
* Keep them short. Writing out a long quotation wastes valuable time.
* Use them to support your comments, not to replace them.
* Don't use them to repeat what you have said.
* Make sure you copy them accurately.
* Enclose quotations in speech (quotation) marks.
* If possible, enclose them in a sentence:

    MacDowall's taunt, 'You're nowt like brothers,' is the last straw for Billy, and he runs at him.

* If you want to use a longer quotation it should be set out on a separate line, introduced by a colon or a comma:

    Unlike the other teachers, Mr Farthing is quick to praise, trying to bring out the best from everyone: 'Very good, Anderson. Thank you. Now has anyone else anything interesting to tell us?'

## Close reference to the text

Besides quoting you should also make close reference to the novel. For example:

> Jud has got bullying down to a fine art. He uses his strength to dominate Billy whenever he gets the chance. For example, he thumps him in the kidneys for reminding him about the alarm, tears his book from his hand, hurling it across the room, and clutches Billy in a half-nelson to make him reveal where he found the kestrel.

# Sample essays

## Question 1

**Discuss the roles of Mr Sugden and Mr Farthing in *A Kestrel for a Knave*.**

### Grade C essay

1 Relevant introduction

Barry Hines is interested in education, especially in secondary modern schools at the time, so Mr Sugden and Mr Farthing are important characters. As teachers they have a responsibility to do their best for their pupils and to set them a good example.[1]

2 Inaccurate quotation
3 Spelling mistake

Mr Sugden the games teacher seems to think mostly about the impression he makes on others. In his smart club colours and football boots 'polished as black as the bombs used by assassins in comic strips'[2] he is not realy[3] interested in the boys. He wants to show how well he can play, and organises the way games are played for this purpose. He has no use for anyone who doesn't like or isn't good at football.

4 Short quotation
5 Apostrophe missing
6 Close reference to the text

He is a bully from the start, making Billy wear vast shorts and laughing at his poor vocabulary. On the pitch he makes it clear he doesn't want Billy in his team and sends him into goal though he knows Billy hates it. When Billy lets in a goal Mr Sugden kicks a ball hard at him, accusing him of 'slack work'[4]. He does not applaud Billy with the boys when he swings from the goalpost bars and makes a perfect gymnasts[5] landing.[6]

7 More detail needed

Even with the boys who do like football Mr Sugden is threatening. He asks Tibbut if he would prefer going to maths.[7]

8 Clumsy expression

He doesn't play very well but thinks he does and does[8] anything to win, even cheating and giving goals and penalties to his own team.

9 Personal response

None of this is right for a teacher, who ought to set a good example to his pupils. That's partly why they are there.[9]

Mr Sugden is even worse in the shower room when he makes Billy stand under the cold shower and then admits he did it because Billy made him lose the match. Even the boys protest, but Mr Sugden takes no notice.

It's not surprising there's so much bullying in the school if that's the example he sets to the boys.[10]

**10 Personal response**

Mr Farthing is the opposite to Mr Sugden. I think Barry Hines wants us to see both sides of school life, even if he does disapprove of secondary modern education.[11]

**11 Reference to author's aims**

He is liked and respected by the boys although he can be tough on them like his threatening to punish them all if Billy can't think of something to talk about.[12]

**12 Clumsy expression and poor punctuation**

Unlike Mr Sugden he seems to enjoy teaching, and puts the boys[13] interests first. He seems sympathetic when Billy comes in with his hands hurting and tries to make him take part. He encourages and often praises him. 'Well done, Billy,' [14] he says, using his first name instead of the usual Casper. When the class applaud Billy he lets them finish before returning to the lesson. He tries to encourage the boys by offering a reward for finding a word in the dictionary.[15]

**13 Apostrophe missing**

**14 Short quotation**

**15 No clear links between points**

Billy tells him later that he's the only master he can talk to, and the only teacher who doesn't treat them like morons. 'They're allus callin' us idiots and numbskulls,' he complains.[16]

**16 Quotation**

Later, after he stops the fight between MacDowall and Billy he listens sympathetically to Billy.[17] He ends up asking if he can watch Billy and Kes during the lunch hour. I can't imagine Mr Sugden asking this.[18]

**17 More detail needed**

**18 Personal response**

When he does watch Kes he is full of admiration for her beauty and Billy's skill. He doesn't mind Billy telling him that he must move slowly and be quiet. He accepts that Billy's the boss[19] in that situation.

**19 Colloquialism**

Mr Farthing is also interested in what Billy is going to do when he leaves school. That's more than Mr Gryce is.[20]

**20 Clumsy expression**

**21 Personal response, but clearer reference to theme of education would be useful**

Mr Sugden and Mr Farthing are important in the novel because they show the best and worst side of teachers. I'd certainly rather be taught by Mr Farthing than Mr Sugden.[21]

**Grade A\* essay**

Barry Hines has always been interested in social issues. In *A Kestrel for a Knave* he focuses on the divisive system of education in the 1960s. Boys 'passing' the 11+ exam went to grammar school, while those like Billy Casper who 'failed' usually went to a secondary modern. Of course there were good schools, but too often both the teachers and the level of education were of inferior quality. Hines feels strongly that children like Billy were victims of an unequal education system. For this reason education is an important theme in the novel.

*1 Clear extended introduction to the topic*

The author introduces Mr Sugden, the games master, and Mr Farthing, who teaches English, as examples of the worst and best kind of teacher. Their responsibilities should include encouragement, stimulus and the pursuit of high standards of behaviour.[1]

*2 Short quotation*
*3 Short quotation*

Mr Sugden is interested in none of these. He is a bully who penalises untalented or unwilling players. He dislikes Billy, who dares to say 'I don't like football,'[2] and enjoys finding fault. Quick to accuse Billy of 'skyving',[3] he mocks his limited vocabulary and forces him to wear outsize shorts. On the field he viciously slams a ball at him for letting in a goal, merely saying, 'Slack work, lad. Slack work.'[4]

*4 Short quotation*

*5 Short quotation*

Billy is, in fact, athletic and agile, but Mr Sugden is blind to this. The boys applaud his perfect athlete's swing down from the goal, but 'Sugden silenced it'.[5] A more perceptive teacher would recognise that Billy's physical agility suggests he could be a competent footballer.

*6 Close reference to the text*
*7 Personal response*

For Mr Sugden, winning is everything. All his energies are directed towards a display of his own prowess and winning the match by any methods. He declares that his side will play downhill, takes first pick when selecting the team, threatens his opponents, grabs their shirts and, as referee as well as player, allows penalties and goals favouring his side.[6] This is no way to encourage good sportsmanship.[7]

Mainly, Mr Sugden asserts his authority with bullying tactics, even threatening to send one of his best players off the field for questioning a decision. In the shower room, however, he reveals a sadistic streak, shamelessly getting his revenge for Billy letting in the last goal. Relishing the sight of Billy forced to stand under the cold sprays, he retorts to the boys' protest: 'If he thinks I'm running

8 Quotation

my blood to water for ninety minutes, and then having the game deliberately thrown away at the last minute, he's another think coming!'[8]

9 Personal response

A man such as Mr Sugden should not be in charge of children.[9] Sadly, he is not the only member of the staff to indulge in bullying. Mr Gryce, the headmaster, is another, and he does not set a good example to his staff.

10 Quotation

Besides representing the classic bully, Mr Sugden has another role in the novel. He provides much of the humour, although unknowingly. In his violet tracksuit bedecked with badges, and his boots 'polished as black and shiny as the bombs used by assassins in comic strips',[10] he is a caricature of a keen sportsman. Lacking a sense of humour, he is unaware of the boys' sly teasing. Nor does he realise their impatience with his failing football skills.

11 Short quotation

'He's like a chuffing carthorse,'[11] says one disgruntled boy.

12 Personal response

Mr Sugden's absurd attempt to combine the role of player, teacher and commentator in the so-called league match is pure comedy. It is a bright moment in a bleak portrait of school life.[12]

While Mr Sugden is totally negative in his approach to teaching, Mr Farthing is positive. He appears to have a vocation, and is the kind of person needed to offset people like Mr Sugden. He is respected, maintaining a relaxed relationship with the boys.

13 Quotation
14 Short quotation

Mr Farthing greets Billy sympathetically after his beating and tries to involve him in the lesson, although his threat of class punishment seems harsh. He uses Billy's talk to expand everyone's vocabulary, and prompts Billy when he falters. As Billy says, later, 'You do at least try to learn us summat',[13] unlike most of the masters who regard 4C as 'idiots, an' numbskulls'.[14]

15 Short quotations

Farthing also tailors his lessons to suit his pupils' abilities and offers incentives. Teaching a weak stream, he constantly reaffirms what they have learnt and is quick to praise. 'Very good, Anderson,' he says after the tale of the tadpoles, and 'Well done, Billy,'[15] (using his first name) when Billy concludes the first part of his talk. According to Billy, such praise is rare.

Although he is unaware of its importance, Mr Farthing is responsible for getting the boys to write a tall story. This gives us a valuable insight into Billy's life and his yearning for a better one.

Mr Farthing is not only concerned with his pupils in the classroom. He hates bullying, and pounces on MacDowall at break before demonstrating what it feels like.[16] (Other teachers might have left them to sort out the fight themselves.)[17]

16 Clumsy expression
17 Personal response

He listens sympathetically to Billy afterwards, and wants to know why he always seems 'to cop it'.[18] He agrees he was harsh with Billy after his beating—an admission many teachers would not make—and asks about his home life and his plans for when he leaves school. We cannot imagine Mr Sugden showing such an interest.[19]

18 Short quotation

19 Personal response

Nor can we imagine Mr Sugden giving up his lunch break to watch Billy fly Kes, though Mr Farthing makes it clear that the privilege is his. He accepts Billy's authority without question. 'I won't breathe,'[20] he promises when told where to stand.

20 Short quotation

Their conversation afterwards, like that at the end of break, is very important to our understanding of Billy, who finds he can relax with Mr Farthing in a way that he cannot do with any other adult except, perhaps, the farmer.

Mr Farthing is not only the kind of teacher everyone would like to have, he is also perhaps the nearest to a father-figure that Billy has known since his own father left home. Billy's lack of rewarding relationships in his daily life must partly account for his behaviour, his frustrations and his rebellious attitude towards adults.[21]

21 Personal response

Barry Hines's sympathies with Billy stem partly from the fact that he seems never to have had a chance in life. He is not happy at home, and school offers him very little to compensate. Hines feels strongly that Billy, and boys like him, have been let down by the education system. While acknowledging that there are inspiring teachers like Mr Farthing in the profession, he feels the need to expose the darker side of school life which destroys self-esteem and offers nothing in return.[22]

22 Strong conclusion rounds off discussion and returns to the author's intentions

This essay answers the question fully, with evidence of personal involvement and a good understanding of the topic. Frequent quotations and close reference to the text support the argument. The essay is well expressed and free from spelling mistakes.

## Question 2

**Billy is a liar, a thief and a rebel, yet he engages our sympathy. Why do you think this is?**

Grade C essay

1 Relevant introduction

Billy may be a liar, a thief and a rebel, but there is much more to him than that. He is someone who has struck out for himself to learn new skills, overcoming all sorts of difficulties. He also comes from an unsatisfactory background with no one to set him a good example.[1]

2 Short quotation
3 Colloquialism

It must be hard for Billy, coming from a home like his. His father has gone, and he misses him dreadfully. His mother doesn't much care for him, and goes out most nights leaving him on his own. Jud seems to enjoy bullying him by showing he's stronger, and trying to annoy him. 'What's up wi' thee, shit t'bed?'[2] he asks when Billy comes down early. And there's not much money around.[3]

Perhaps Billy's father would have been a good influence on him, but he left home when Billy was quite small, and Mrs Casper is too busy enjoying herself to think about such things. She is certainly not a good example, as she brings men home for the night, swears at Billy, isn't interested in what he does when she's not there. She bullies him sometimes too.

4 Quotation
5 Clumsy expression

Billy resents that he's expected to do most of the house chores. He complains to Kes, 'I'm fed up o' being chased about. There's allus somebody after me'.[4] So he's rebellious.[5]

6 Short quotation
7 Quotation
8 Poor punctuation
9 Personal response

School isn't much better. Most of the teachers look down on Billy's class, calling them 'idiots, an' numbskulls'[6] and Billy doesn't like it. 'When there's any trouble, they pick on me 'cos I'm t'littlest,'[7] he tells Mr Farthing. Here are more reasons for being rebellious,[8] I don't think we blame him.[9]

10 Spelling mistake

11 Clumsy expression

There is as much bullying at school as there is at home, from boys like MacDowl[10] as well as teachers like Mr Gryce and Mr Sugden. No one stamps on it. They can't really if the head teacher doesn't set an example and he's one of the worst.[11]

12 Spelling mistake
13 Close reference to the text, but clumsy sentence
14 Short quotation

Billy dosen't[12] steal for the sake of it. He's hungry twice, because he's had no breakfast or dinner, and the third time he has tried to borrow a book from the library but hasn't.[13] 'I want a book today',[14] he says, so he goes to the local bookshop and steals one. He

shouldn't have done this, but with a brother who tells him he's 'crackers'[15] to steal something that isn't money, it's not surprising that thieving comes to him so easily. No one at home tells him off.[16]

15 Short quotation

16 Colloquialism

In spite of what Jud says about stealing money, he is furious when Billy takes his. He doesn't mean to steal it at first, but hearing that Jud's double bet is unlikely to win he decides to spend it on himself. If Billy is very guilty he certainly gets what he deserves, for it leads to Kes's death. He does not understand what the win would mean to Jud, and it seems a harsh punishment.[17]

17 Personal response

As far as lying is concerned, lots of people lie to try to get out of trouble, even grown-ups. With Mr Gryce and the rest of the teachers after him all the time it's natural.[18] Billy does lie at other times too, though, like with Jud about his book, and Kes.[19] But these lies don't hurt anyone.

18 Personal response
19 More detail needed; clumsy expression

The great thing about Billy is the way he no longer goes around with the gang vandilising[20] the estate, but spends his time with Kes, looking after, training her. He had to overcome reading problems and be very patient. He always puts Kes first. This is why we sympathise with him whatever else he might have done, for he has lost everything.[21]

20 Spelling mistake

21 Personal response
22 Spelling mistake
23 Conclusion makes new point and shows personal response, but the ending is weak

If Billy had a different background he might not have rebelled, felt the need to steal, or to lie. We should remember that. I think what he acheives[22] with Kes is amazing, and he deserves our sympathy for everything.[23]

## Grade A* essay

1 Thoughtful intro-duction indicating treatment of the topic

Before we can discuss why we sympathise with Billy in spite of his faults, we need to consider to what extent he is to blame for his behaviour. We must think about his background, especially at home and at school, the way it has influenced his development, and to what extent it might bear some of the responsibility.[1]

2 Quotation

Billy seems to have had a secure life before his father left home. His tall story, and the flashback in the final episode, imply that he misses his father greatly. His memory of 'Whispering questions up to his dad; his dad leaning down to answer them,'[2] does not sound very special, but there is no such relationship between him and his mother. Since his father's departure there has been no one to whom he relates in the same way, and no one to give him moral guidance.

Mrs Casper is an unreliable mother in all respects. With her reduced income she can no longer afford home comforts and she is not to blame for this, but she is slovenly and a bad manager. She is totally self-absorbed, uninterested in Billy, not caring what he does in his free time.

She is certainly not a good example to a teenager. She tries to bribe him to go shopping for her: 'I'll give you a tanner,'[3] she says, but she quickly becomes foul-mouthed. 'I'll bloody murder you when I get hold of you,'[4] she threatens when he refuses to go.

Apart from the the final flashback there are many other hints that Billy longs for a better life. He dislikes his mother bringing men home for the night, and resents the way she treats him. 'Do this, do that, I've to do everything in the house,'[5] he complains to Kes.

The neat, clean shed, contrasting with his untidy home, and his envious glimpse of the comfortable house on his paper round, with a happy middle-class family waved off by their mother, is further evidence that in better circumstances Billy might be a different person. We sympathise with his situation.[6]

Billy has drifted, rather than grown up, in an unstable, uncaring background. Left alone at night when his mother went out, he joined the gang vandalising the estate. Violence of different sorts has become an everyday occurrence for him.

His brother Jud could hardly be a worse example. An aggressive bully, he victimises Billy at every opportunity, thumping him in the kidneys, mocking his plans to train a kestrel, and taking cruel revenge on him through Kes. He is abusive to his mother, and to Mrs Rose when he learns about the bet.[7] It is little wonder that Billy is undisciplined.

Except for Mr Farthing, who respects the boys, and is respected in turn, there is little at school to redress the balance. Bullying is endemic. Punishments are frequent, brutal and often unfair. Low achievers are derided by most of the staff. Billy tells Mr Farthing that they call them 'idiots, an' numbskulls, an' cretins'.[8] They make no attempt to teach them anything. He adds that when there's any trouble he's always picked on, ''cos I'm t'littlest'.[9]

It is not surprising that Billy is rebellious nor that, like many people of all ages, he lies to avoid trouble. This is, perhaps, excusable at

*Marginal notes:*

3 Short quotation

4 Short quotation

5 Quotation

6 Personal response

7 Close reference to the text

8 Quotation

9 Short quotation

| | |
|---|---|
| 10 Short quotation | school with its punishment-based regime. But he also lies to Jud, saying 'I've lent'[10] the book, and he tells Mr Farthing that he found Kes on the ground. However, these lies are evasive rather than damaging to others. |
| 11 Close reference to text | But Billy's stealing is another matter. His poacher's pocket suggests that he has always been a petty thief. He deftly removes chocolate bars from Mr Porter's counter, and orange juice and eggs from the milkman.[11] There are some grounds for sympathy here, for there was no breakfast at home. |
| 12 Quotation<br>13 Personal response | His theft of *The Falconer's Handbook* is rather different. Courteous and persuasive, Billy does his best to borrow a book legally. But his impatience rules his actions. 'I don't want to wait that long,' he says, when told he must return to the library on Monday. 'I want a book today.'[12] He should not steal, but we sympathise with his enthusiasm.[13] |
| 14 Quotation | It is ironical that, in the end, the only person Billy really harms through stealing is his brother. Yet Jud has shown no disapproval of Billy's theft of the book. 'I could understand it if it wa' money,' he says, 'but chuff me, not a book.'[14] Here is another example of corrupting standards of behaviour. |
| 15 Good example of showing both sides of the argument<br>16 Personal response | Billy should have placed Jud's bet, but there is no malice in his actions. He behaves honestly by his own standards, deciding to go ahead after gambling with himself. It is only when he learns that it seems like a bad bet that he spends the money on himself. Again, hunger is partly the reason, for he has missed his lunch to look after Kes.[15] Jud's vindictive revenge is a far greater punishment than Billy deserves, and we share Billy's grief.[16] |
| 17 Personal response<br>18 Quotation | Balanced with Billy's faults are his virtues, which surely outweigh the former.[17] He has left the gang with its antisocial influence and has created a new world for himself. He has overcome his reading problems to learn all he can about falconry, and spent long hours patiently training Kes. He can now fly her free. 'Well that was it. I'd done it,' he tells the class proudly, 'I'd trained her'.[18] |
| 19 Good comparison | Billy is likeable: ready to be friendly, funny and irreverent. He is observant, imaginative and interested in nature. This is partly why we warm to him. He will, perhaps, always remain untameable, like Kes.[19] But in his training of her he has made the first step towards accepting responsibility for his own actions. |

Our sympathy with Billy lies mainly in his loss of Kes. But we also feel for his situation as underdog, a product of a broken home, and a victim of circumstances. He will probably end up down the mine.

20 Conclusion includes new point and shows personal response, with reasons for our sympathy with Billy

Opinions vary on who should be blamed for juvenile misconduct. Some say the children, others say their parents. Some suggest that the problem lies with neither, but in their environment. Billy has had a poor start in life, with little help to put him on the right path. For this, if no other reason, he engages our sympathy.[20]

There is a strong personal response here. The argument is well expressed and supported with detailed evidence in the form of quotations and close reference to the text. There are no spelling errors.

# How to get an A* grade

To get an A* grade you must:

* make a full, perceptive and personal response to the given task
* show insight into the author's ideas and purposes
* show a clear understanding of language, form and structure
* support your argument with detailed analysis and evidence
* express yourself in clear, formal English, in an appropriate tone
* spell accurately.

**Review your learning**

(Answers are given on page 83.)

1 What is the difference between higher-tier and foundation-tier questions?
2 What must you do besides telling the story?
3 On which aspects of *A Kestrel for a Knave* do GCSE questions usually focus?
4 What two ways are suggested for making essay plans?
5 Which two kinds of evidence should you use in your essay?
6 What might you include in an introduction?
7 What might you include in a conclusion?

# Answers

Answers to 'Review your learning' questions.

## Context (page 11)

1 A neighbour saw him on the coalface and asked if he couldn't find a better job.
2 The falcon family (*Falconidae*).
3 His brother reared and trained a kestrel, and Hines was closely involved.
4 A kestrel was thought to be difficult to train, and humans could not eat its quarry.
5 They must take a course and obtain a licence.
6 They thought of themselves, and were regarded as, failures; they usually received an inferior standard of education; they mostly left school without any qualifications.
7 Many houses had been damaged or destroyed by bombs; people expected better living conditions; slums were torn down, and new factories and other industries needed homes for their workers.
8 This is a subjective question that only you can answer, but you might wish to talk about the visual impact and the imagery in each poem.

## Plot and structure (page 28)

1 Short episodes rather than longer chapters give the impression of time passing swiftly towards the climax at the end of the day.
2 They enable Barry Hines to put the past into the framework of the present, and thus widen the scope of the main narrative.
3 Episode 21, when Billy spends Jud's money on himself instead of the bet.
4 A young falcon or hawk taken from the nest for training.
5 Fish and chips, cigarettes and a box of matches. (The butcher gives him the meat free.)
6 A goshawk.
7 Mrs Rose.
8 This is a subjective question. You may think that Billy asks for trouble because he is not prepared to fit in at home, on the estate, in school or among his

friends. You may feel that he is picked on and bullied because he is small for his age and a known troublemaker. Whether you think he deserves to be in trouble is a matter of opinion, but you should base your view on evidence in the text and try to be analytical.

9 There is no correct answer to this question, but you should explain the reasons for your choice, bearing in mind that two contrasting episodes will give a potential reader a clearer impression of the novel than two that are similar in content or setting.

You may also think that, although the last chapter is the most powerful, it would be a pity to disclose the ending.

# Characterisation (page 45)

1 Mr Porter.
2 Tibbut.
3 Jud has stolen his bicycle.
4 Jud thinks he's 'crackers' to steal a book. He would understand if it had been money.
5 He believes that Billy is genuinely interested in the kestrels and does not intend to harm them.
6 Her character is not fully developed. We see only one side of her personality, and her reactions are always predictable.
7 He thinks they:
   * are superficial, interested only in their '*gear*' and their music, with 'nothing solid beneath'
   * have no respect for authority
   * run to their fathers for support when punished
   * have no guts or backbone
   * are 'just fodder for the mass media'
8 The messenger's appearance:
   * confirms Billy's earlier comment that Mr Gryce never listens to anyone, and shows him as lacking perception. He should have realised that the boy is an unlikely smoker, and that his unrelaxed hand indicates he is unused to being caned
   * reveals the smokers as contemptible. First they make the boy take their incriminating evidence, then they menace him with threatening expressions when he tries to speak up
9 Your sympathies may lie with one or both. You could argue that the librarian is obliged to observe the rules strictly, making no exceptions. Or you may feel that Billy's interest should be fostered and his polite persistence rewarded with a compromise, such as reading the book on the premises.

# Themes (page 56)

1  An idea, image or train of thought running through a narrative. The intertwined themes provide the skeleton of the novel.
2  The four different facets of Billy's environment: home, urban, natural and school.
3  Kes is a symbol of Billy's individuality and his independent spirit. Like Billy, she is trained, not tamed.
4  There is no 'correct' answer to this question.
5  There are two main aspects to this:
    * At a symbolic level, Billy's life at home and at school lacks warmth in an emotional sense. When Kes is killed his only source of emotional comfort is destroyed.
    * Billy is small for his age, and skinny. He feels the cold partly because of his physique, and partly because his mother does not provide adequate clothing. His home is inadequately heated because Mrs Casper is not a good house-keeper and spends her money going out instead of on essentials such as fuel.
6  Episode 2 gives a bird's eye view of the general layout of the area where Billy lives, with the estate amongst other landmarks. Episodes 21 and 26 provide detailed descriptions of the estate where Billy has grown up. They emphasise the dreary sameness of the housing, the vandalism and the dilapidation. They explain, partly, why Billy is as he is.
7  Your map may not be quite like anyone else's, but you should be able to sketch the main features of the area. You might like to ask a friend to do it too, and compare versions.

# Style (page 64)

1  The narrator speaks objectively, with no indication of personal reactions or feelings.
2  Mr Farthing uses Standard English; Billy mostly uses local dialect.
3  The 1960s, in South Yorkshire.
4  It is used to criticise the educational system at the time, and shows up the failure of many urban estates to provide a decent standard of living.
5  The Beatles.
6  A simile makes a direct comparison, usually introduced by the words *like* or *as*. A metaphor compares two things by stating that one thing *is* another.
7  Hines never states directly who is speaking, though he sometimes indicates this indirectly. He rarely suggests how people speak, leaving it to the reader to infer tone of voice from diction, spelling and punctuation.
8  Much of the imagery in the novel reveals Billy's personal view of his world. For example, he likens the kindling paper balls to hydrangea flowers (Episode 2),

sees Jud as a sleeping monster (Episode 8), the trees at the edge of the wood as a curtain (Episode 9) and the potholes outside the betting shop as bomb craters (Episode 21). This insight into Billy's response to his surrounding shows him as sensitive and imaginative. Some of the games he plays are an extension of these qualities.

9 Your notes might include:
  * '12.15 p.m.' — throughout the novel Hines makes the reader aware of the passing hours of Billy's day
  * short crisp sentences — underlining Billy's frustration
  * in contrast, a long, flowing sentence describing Sugden's attempts to keep up, and the ease with which the boys accelerate past him
  * repetition of 'jump', 'tick' and 'blind' for emphasis
  * onomatopoeia — 'Tick tick tick tick'
  * simile — Sugden 'sweating like a drayhorse'
  * short, violent exclamations using oaths and swear-words for a realistic tone

# Tackling the exam (page 79)

1 Higher-tier questions have few or no guidelines. Foundation-tier questions give pointers to help candidates plan their answers.
2 Demonstrate your knowledge and understanding in a personal response to the question.
3 Plot, character and theme.
4 Making bullet-point notes or a spider diagram.
5 Quotations and close reference to the text.
6 Your interpretation of the question; a brief summary of how you are going to approach your answer; one or two general but relevant comments.
7 Summarising your argument; making a general comment; introducing a new, but relevant, idea.

# References

*The Times*, 5 November 2005, 'A Yorkshire boy still working close to the coal face' (Barry Hines interviewed by Carol Midgley).

Afterword by Barry Hines to *A Kestrel for a Knave*, Penguin Classics, 2000.

Quotation from an interview with David Bradley (who acted Billy Casper in the film), from www.geocities.com/freycinette/Kes

Cocker, C. and Mabey, R. (2005) *Birds Britannica*, Chatto & Windus.

Hopkins, G. M. 'The Windhover' from *Poems and Prose of Gerard Manley Hopkins*, Penguin Books (1953).

Hughes, T. (1967) 'The Hawk in the Rain' from *The Hawk in the Rain*, Faber and Faber.

Lascelles, G. (1892) *The Badminton Library of Sports and Pastimes: Coursing and Falconry*, Longman, Green & Co.

Peterson, R., Mountfort, G. and Hollom, P. A. D. (1958) *A Field Guide to the Birds of Britain and Europe* (3rd edn revised), Collins.

White, T. H. *The Goshawk*, Jonathan Cape, 1951; Penguin Books, 1963.